ROD STEIGER

ROD STEIGER

Memoirs of a Friendship

Tom Hutchinson

Foreword by Ray Bradbury

FROMM INTERNATIONAL
NEW YORK

First Fromm International Edition, 2000

Copyright © Tom Hutchinson 1998

Poems and Pieces copyright © Rod Steiger 1998

Foreword copyright © Ray Bradbury 1998

Library of Congress Cataloging-in-Publication Data is available.

ISBN 0-88064-253-X

Manufactured in the United States of America.

John Walker was my saviour and shaping arbiter in assembling these reminiscences. Saints of patience were my editors and my agent who had such faith. Rod Steiger is the icon I have tried to make human.

To them all my gratitude, and to others too numerous to mention. They know who they are – and how grateful I am to them. And that, dear friends, will have to suffice.

I owe heartfelt thanks not only to Rod Steiger, who supplied me with most of the photographs, but to the British Film Institute and the National Film Theatre for letting me have the transcript of Steiger's lecture to the NFT. The usual gratitude is offered to the film studios for whom Rod worked – from United Artists, via Paramount to MGM – besides others, and to Ruth Jacobs and photographer Chris Cornwell of London's Langham Hilton.

No inadequacy of acknowledgement is intentional. But if there is any such inadequacy it will be rectified in the next edition.

My dedication is to my wife, Pat.

Rod Steiger's dedication is to Anna and Michael.

Contents

Foreword

You do not introduce Rod Steiger. You light the fuse and stand aside.

I remember one of our first collisions thirty years ago, when Rod drove up in front of our house in a spanking new Jaguar twelve-cylinder beauty, jumped out and yelled to us, 'Eat your heart out!'

Simultaneously I recall how our friendship began one night, thirty-five years ago, at James Whitmore's Santa Monica Canyon home. Introduced for the first time, we talked on until two in the morning. You name the subject, we took off its skin and settled its hash. From then on there were intermittent dinners, lunches, theatre dates and visits to Hollywood movie sets. You name it, Rod had an opinion. But then I am absolutely the same. We were a counterbalanced, opinionated, but friendly duo.

When Jack Smight called me wanting to buy the rights to my book *The Illustrated Man*, I said, yes, he could buy them – *if* he hired one of the actors on my shortlist: Paul Newman, Burt Lancaster and, you've guessed it, Rod Steiger. A week later Rod called me with the news: 'Smight wants me to appear in *The Illustrated Man*. And he wants Claire to be with me.' Two talents, Rod and his wife Claire Bloom, for the price of one.

I called Smight immediately and said, 'Buy the rights!'

With mixed results. The performances by Rod and Claire were fine, the photography lovely, the music by Jerry Goldsmith superb, but the screenplay was stranded out in some New Jersey cowpatch.

Rod came to me during the first week of photography and said, 'Have you read this screenplay?'

'No,' I replied.

'Why not?' Rod asked.

'Nobody asked me to read it,' I said. 'I want the courtesy of someone wanting a response from me. No one asked, so there was no response.'

'Do you mind if I rewrite the script, day by day?' Rod said.

'Bless you,' I said. 'Whatever you do will be better than what's there. Be my guest.'

So, as the weeks passed, Rod did what he could to aerate and align the garbled words. He did not, of course, fully succeed. It was a job for a true screenwriter. There was none, including myself, at hand.

The opening night of *The Illustrated Man* was at a cinema near my house. When it was all over and my fans left the theatre, dejected, a nine-year-old boy approached me and, looking up at me with a pale face, said, 'Mr Bradbury. What *happened*?'

'Nothing,' I said. 'Nothing at all.'

To counter despair with celebration I bring up the memory of *In the Heat of the Night*. I lunched with Rod and Sidney Poitier, and saw that the film was headed in absolutely the right direction.

The following year when it was nominated for an Academy Award, fearing that the film might be neglected by the voting members, I prepared a bottle of Mumm's champagne with my own awards plastered all over it and dropped it by Rod's house, telling the maid to stash it in the fridge – just in case.

My gesture was not needed. At the awards ceremony that night, Rod's name was announced and he walked out to seize his Oscar.

I had heard rumours that over the years, playing fast and hard at tennis, Rod sometimes yelled at his opponents, the same sort of yell he had flung at my wife and myself all that time ago. In his moment of triumph I half expected and half hoped he might lift his Oscar high and shout across the tennis net, or up from his new Jag, 'Eat your heart out!'

He earned and deserved it. What could have been better?

Ray Bradbury

Introduction

Rod Steiger was loaded when he came to spend Christmas Day with us in the mid-seventies. Not only was he stooped under the growing weight of Hollywood celebrity, but he was laden with gifts as a kind of passport and introduction to our festive cliché of family.

He had rung up on the morning of Christmas Eve to tell us that he was in London – and alone. For some reason he couldn't be with his daughter, Anna Justine, his beloved child by former wife, actress Claire Bloom. And there was no other woman to minister to him. He is a man who likes ministry, and there was Pat, my wife, whom he has always insisted on formalizing as Patricia. (That way he thinks he is putting on his Sunday-best Christmas accent just for her. He's very polite like that.)

So, of course, we invited him for Christmas lunch, remembering that he had once told us that Christmas was usually an unhappy affair for him. When he was a child his mother went out on a three-day alcohol binge over Yule and left him alone with a bereft Christmas tree and an even emptier heart. We could but try to give him a good time.

There were, of course, Christmas rituals to go through, Pat told him – carols to sing, funny hats to be worn, presents to be opened after the meal. 'I know all about that,' he grumbled. 'Not that I always do them.' This time he had to, he was told. Even superstars had to conform.

Chauffeur-driven, he arrived on the sliced-fine stroke of noon.

15

The driver came in, had a drink and then went away to his own celebrations. Steiger drank to each and every one of us and we were off on the annual journey of enjoying our family's company, this time though with a superstar along for the ride. We drank La Tache, a red wine he always insisted on buying me, although I once found out how much it cost and, disconcerted, realized it amounted to nearly as much as my second mortgage. I didn't refuse it, though.

Years later he was to relate his account of the meal to his fourth wife, Paula.

'Yeah, we had all the trimmings – roast goose and Christmas pudding, that sort of thing. Yeah, goose! Not that the grown-ups saw much of it. Those three kids of theirs dived in as though they hadn't eaten for years. Perhaps they hadn't, I don't know.

'They were terribly polite about it, you know, in that very English way that takes its hat off before it knocks you down and boots you. That goose vanished as quickly as anything at the Cratchits'. I remember being asked if I wanted another slice of goose. I scarcely remember having one. You know, Paula, the Hutchinson hunger is legendary.'

We had honoured Rod Steiger by treating him as though he were a human being. It was something he remembered for years after. So did we. The man who came to dinner . . . and stayed on.

We played Christmas music and Steiger, echoing the vocals he had as poor Judd in *Oklahoma!*, hummed along with it. Simple, corny things like that. And then we were into late afternoon and opening our gifts to each other. Steiger had bought his presents at the last moment: they were all expensive pens. My sons promised to pass examinations with them; our daughter did the same, only she had an extra treat. Remembering that she is left-handed, as he is, Steiger had bought her a book, *The Natural Superiority of the Left-Handed*.

We started talking about the word 'sinister' and how it was associated with being left-handed and how this applied to

Steiger's serial killer in the film *No Way to Treat a Lady*. I had liked the film's screenplay because it was clever enough to make you understand that both the killer and George Segal, the pursuing detective, were Momma's boys. 'More than I ever was in real life,' said Steiger, as though to himself. It cast a chill over the warmth.

After that we put on funny hats and sank into Christmas afternoon apathy, a languor only broken by the recital of Steiger's audio-visual jokes:

'Welcome to this tour of the castle, ladies and gentlemen. As you see, luxurious gardens reach out to a golden sunset. The hedges are a marvel of majestic topiary. And there is his lordship at the archery butts, putting in a morning's practice. A marvellous—'

There was a 'THUNK' from Steiger and he would gaze down with solemn bewilderment at his chest from which, we imagined, a sudden arrow had sprouted.

There was always applause at these 'audio-visuals'. Ever in search of an audience Steiger responded, 'I thought the timing was off, but it seems to have worked.'

One of the children said that even without a beard he seemed like Santa Claus. Always conscious of his weight, Steiger grumbled, 'I doubt I could get down your chimney. I'm more used to hotels.'

About five o'clock in the afternoon the chauffeur arrived back to take him to his West End hotel and his solitary suite. Oh, yes, it was one of the best Christmas Days he had ever spent, he said, eyes leaking a little. Steiger is a man who can weep at the slightest provocation. He had, it seems, been mightily provoked.

Christmas is a time of odours. From roasting poultry to the moistened spice of pudding. Now the smell of Rod's cigar – which he had tried to smoke but had to keep on taking from his mouth to say something – hung around for days after. Two worlds had collided and merged in a puff of cigar smoke. We returned to our own lives and Rod Steiger to his.

I thought then that I would like to write about Rodney Stephen Steiger and what he has meant to me and my family through the years. I have been in showbusiness as a film critic, TV producer and film columnist all my working, if not waking, life. I had always admired the quality that had made Steiger one of the most important Hollywood stars. He had been able to walk the tightrope of his drama, juggling personalities – Napoleon, Mussolini, mass murderers . . .

Oh, yes, and I've criticized him. When he made *The Specialist* with Sylvester Stallone, in which he was a language-mangling Godfather, I deplored the film's subject. Stallone's character, the hero, detonated explosives. Having had two IRA bombs go off fifty yards from my home – each in the opposite direction – I considered it irresponsible entertainment to idealize a bomber. Steiger looked lost and dejected. 'I never thought of that,' he said.

For most of us on this side of the business, actors rarely become friends, because we spend too little time with them. There is a story about the American actress, Anne Bancroft, who got angry with her husband, the comedian Mel Brooks, because he was teasing her while she was preparing for a scene. 'Do not interfere with THE INSTRUMENT!' she yelled. She was referring to her body which she had trained and controlled to respond to dramatic situations, in the way a virtuoso tunes a cello or violin.

That instrument – the body and the space surrounding it – is precious and inviolate, and the hem and aura of a garment that must not be walked on by outsiders. That is why, in interviews, journalists are allowed only so far and no further.

With Rod Steiger I got closer. We became friends. That is because of a paradox. In one way he is more secure than other stars, in another he is vulnerable and needs concern from others.

Add to that the fact that we forget how lonely it can be if you are a stranger in a strange land – a visitor from abroad who, once the glad-handers and the professional greeters have gone, finds the world to be a cold, excluding place.

He asked me to go with him when he was to be interviewed on the BBC by an affable interviewer. 'I don't know the guy. I'd be grateful if you would come along.' He also asked me to accompany him to hear his daughter, Anna Justine, who is an opera singer, give a recital. 'I might say the wrong thing to her afterwards. I'm not all that fond of the kind of modern opera she does.' Rod Steiger, who has so often played the outsider in movies, can also find himself outside normal family life and friendship. That Christmas Day was both escape and retreat.

As Christopher Isherwood said, 'We all make our own personal mythologies.' Rod Steiger belongs to our family's. As I understand it, we belong to his. When we first met his fourth and most tender wife, Paula – sadly no longer with him – she said, 'I've heard so much about you all. Rod loves you deeply.'

But, as with all friends, there are things we don't know about each other, so, this is a different sort of biography. I am trying to evoke a relationship which has lasted through many movies and a number of wives, awards and massive depressions. This is my perspective on an actor who throws himself into a role as though off a cliff, still working at pensionable age, keeping his small son in the loving luxury of a Malibu home.

Family is what Rod Steiger has always yearned for during his long, eventful existence. Sadly, he has never been able to achieve it properly. But, perhaps if he had, he might not have been as great an actor as he has become.

PART ONE

STEIGER, STEIGER

- 1 -

For some reason Soho, that raffishly degraded quarter of London, seems to have been a link in our friendship. Rod had an extra ticket to see Laurence Olivier in John Osborne's *The Entertainer* and invited me along. We met, why, I'm not entirely sure, outside a pornographic book shop in Old Compton Street. When I arrived he was staring lugubriously at the advertisements for fetishism and bondage. Oh, the desperate dangers of stardom! He was terrified that some photographer might have taken a picture of him and associated him with such perversities. 'It's dangerous to be out with you, Hutchinson.'

Olivier impressed us both. There is a ferocious moment when Olivier's Archie Rice, the skid-row music-hall comic, slides down the proscenium arch bawling out a blues song on hearing of his son's death in Korea. I could hear Steiger mumbling; I leaned nearer. 'The bastard! The bastard!' muttered Steiger. 'How does he get away with it?' It was the risk Olivier was taking in trying for that proscenium slide that was admired; he might have slithered into bathos. No, he didn't want to go backstage to meet Olivier. 'What could I say to him? He must have known he was pulling off a marvellous stroke of theatre. He doesn't need me.'

It was an interesting contrast of styles. When I worked on the film, *Battle of Britain*, I told Olivier of that night, knowing that Olivier had no truck with the Method style of acting which had created Rod Steiger's stage attitudes. Olivier's film hero was Spencer Tracy, who never seemed to be acting at all, whereas those who came from the Method stable bucked and reared like

23

nervy thoroughbreds. You knew that they were acting, all right. 'Steiger, I like, though,' said Sir Larry. 'He is, for all that malarkey of the Studio, very disciplined.'

'He never bumps into the furniture,' I ventured, remembering Olivier's dictum that actors should learn their lines and never stumble into the furniture.

'Oh, he lets you know the furniture's there all right. But it becomes part of the way he acts and the character he's building. He should have come backstage.' Nobody ever swore as elegantly as Olivier. 'I would have been fucking flattered.'

Taking risks is what Rod Steiger most admires in another actor, because he also is a risk taker. When he saw Marlon Brando in *Last Tango in Paris*, he wanted to rail against him. Instead he said, 'Did you see the wiggle of arse that Brando gave when he left the dance hall? I'll bet that was unrehearsed and yet it gave so much extra to the character. Sure, I still hate the bastard. But you have to admit talent when you see it. And Brando sure has talent.'

Talent was the oxygen required to breathe in those days of the fifties and sixties, when the Method Studio, under the stridently theoretical control of Lee Strasberg, nurtured such young actors as Brando, Steiger, Montgomery Clift and Marilyn Monroe. Sir Michael Redgrave once told me that he had studied there for a short period. 'I don't think they taught me anything I didn't know, apart from being able to efface myself. I felt myself to be invisible while on stage in Clifford Odets' *The Country Girl* – for the first act anyway; I was thinking myself into the background.'

Some actors have the foreground thrust upon them, but Rod Steiger fought to achieve his place in the sun. It was on the shifting deck of a warship in the not-so-peaceful Pacific that Rod took the first step in his transformation from a New Jersey youth, with limited prospects, to an acclaimed actor. It was there, at the age of sixteen, a boy among men preparing for sea-battles against the Japanese, that he stopped using his given name of Rodney. 'Answering the roll-call with Rodney was definitely not

24

so hot. I used to use an extra deep voice in case anyone got the wrong idea.'

Rod Steiger, as a mutual friend has said, is a name that suits its bearer, suggesting as it does a brusque, swaggering masculinity. If it is not the man, then it certainly approximates many of the roles he has played over a career that has lasted nearly fifty years.

Following his birth on 14 April 1925, his mother named him after a Dr Rodney who had delivered him. Only his mother and his first wife, Sally Gracie, were to use the less commanding-sounding Rodney in the years to come.

To be sixteen and playing an active part in the war in the Pacific was the result of young Rodney's desperation to escape from his life and its constant humiliations. His childhood had been a troubled one. His parents, Fred and Lorraine, had worked in showbusiness of a sort – they played roadhouses as a small-time song-and-dance act. Their life had been an itinerant one, moving to where the work was. At the time of Rodney's birth they were living in Westhampton, Long Island.

The marriage was as unsettled as their way of life. The relationship had stalled in Westhampton, and soon after Rodney's arrival Fred walked out, never to return. His mother divorced Fred within a year. So far as he knows, Rod has never even seen his father. The only knowledge he has of him comes from his mother and other relations, and their memories do not always match. He is a shadowy, fugitive figure, but one who has haunted Rod through his life; he has been an invisible presence and unseen influence.

'He was supposed to have been a very attractive rather Latin-looking gentleman, a natural musician – he could play anything – and a great dancer,' says Rod, relying on the memories of relatives. But to his son he remains 'a void. A hole. An emptiness, a blackness, a longing.'

Rod's feelings about his father remain ambivalent. 'If I had met him, if a strange man had come up to me one day and said,

"I'm your father," I don't know if I would have burst into tears or broken his jaw in anger, screaming, "Where were you when I needed you!" I don't know why he never contacted me. He certainly knew once I got lucky and my name started to get in the media that I was around. But I always think of him as a dancing fool, I don't know why: slick and patent leather and Rudolph Valentino.

'I've never had a longing to know him. I don't believe that blood is thicker than water. I tried to find out what he was like. But by the time I'd asked my mother and my aunts and uncles I realized that nobody knew. I wouldn't know him even if we were in the same room.'

Rod's mother, Lorraine, plump, energetic and small, with long auburn hair that reached the middle of her back when she wore it loose, was pretty enough to have been offered a movie contract when Rod was five, but she turned it down for unspecified reasons. Shortly after, an operation on her right knee went wrong and it locked so that she was unable to bend it. 'She managed to walk beautifully, swinging it from the hip, so you hardly noticed it,' says Rod.

She noticed, though. This, remember, was in the days when disablement was considered almost as a physical curse upon the morally afflicted. The pain and the shame of it had their effect; Lorraine began to drink more, and, as time went on, she would drink all day. The daughter of Scottish and German immigrants – 'She made a great sauerkraut', Rod remembers – she had been brought up as a Lutheran, a believer in the austere doctrine that, in a world where all are sinners, worth or effort count for nothing in the long term and salvation is by faith alone. She would inculcate the same stern beliefs into her son, even though by her own standards she fell by the wayside into alcoholism.

Steiger himself recalls, when in his teens, being attracted to the Lutheran Church, preaching a few sermons and making friends with the minister, who saw in the actor-to-be a possible propagandist for the faith. 'I liked the guy very much; I also liked the authority I could exert from the pulpit. But one day I had to tell him that I no longer believed in God or, at any rate, not enough to preach His gospels. The minister, I could tell, was very hurt. But if I had taken up that vocation I know now that I would have condemned myself to a life of misery.'

There were other men in his mother's life. When Rodney could barely walk, she met and married Walter Tours, whom he remembers with affection. 'A big man, big in kindness, big in body, big in spirit. A man who I considered my father, having not known my father.' But Walter, too, was fallible, and disappeared for a time when Rod was still a small boy. He left a note on the kitchen table, saying that he had gone to the corner saloon for a beer, and did not return for more than two years.

Lorraine's drinking got worse. Rod never knew whether she'd be home, or he might return to find the house full of boozed companions:

I remember one of her lady friends was sleeping in a drunken stupor with her legs spread and I lit a match and carefully approached her to try to see underneath the darkness created by the blanket what women were built like. Scared to death, but titillated and fascinated. That match went out and I thought I might burn her, or that my mother would never forgive me.

Lorraine worked when she could, in shops and stores, in an attempt to support herself and her son. When the days of Depression hit, they went on Relief, with the young Rod queueing to collect handouts of day-old bread. They moved from one New Jersey town to another: Irvington, Bloomfield and, lastly, Newark, where they settled long enough for Rod to go to the West Side High School, though he was only to spend a year there. He was a popular boy, the dominant figure in his circle of friends: a capable softball player, an incisive storyteller and an enthusiastic participant in plays and entertainments, where

27

his roles ranged from Father Christmas to George Washington. By the time they moved to Newark he was fifteen, a burly, well-built boy who looked older than his years.

On good days, in the evenings when his school work was done, his mother would sit at their upright piano and play and sing songs from her past, sentimental Tin Pan Alley melodies such as 'Roses of Picardy' and 'Shine On, Harvest Moon'. It was rather a pathetic attempt at home life. On bad days, she drank too much. Rod, returning from school, would hear her screaming and shouting as he walked down the street.

From the age of nine, if his mother was not at home he would wait in fear for the telephone to ring: a call from a saloon telling him to come to collect her and lead her home. 'I remember thinking, one day you're going to do something so good no one will laugh at the name of Steiger again. I think that's what gives my acting some of its intensity,' he says. Once, Steiger and I were lunching when he heard that Sir Charles Chaplin had hired a suite upstairs for a party. 'I must go and pay my respects,' he said. I assumed it was to say 'hello' to the genius who had given Rod's second wife, Claire Bloom, her chance in *Limelight*.

That wasn't the reason. It was because he felt Chaplin's own childhood – with a mother whose mental health had forced Chaplin into an orphanage – mirrored his own. 'I think I know what he went through, because I went through it as well.' Chaplin, by then in his dotage, accepted Steiger's worship, though he was rather confused by its enthusiasm.

One Christmas morning, when Rod was nine, he awoke to discover the house empty. His mother had not arrived home from a drinking binge. The Christmas tree was lying on the floor, and she did not return for three days. The distance of adulthood makes us forget just how painful childhood hurt can be. Children have no yardsticks of experience to go by; the pain seems likely to go on for ever. Steiger was, as he says, his own father and mother.

As a boy, Rod began to write poetry, something he continues

to do, finding in it a release from everyday worries. Gloom invaded those poems like night.

He determined to leave home as fast as he could, which was sooner than he expected. As he was growing up, the US had moved from a position of neutrality towards foreign conflicts to a realization that some sort of involvement in a world war was inevitable. In September 1939, German armies invaded Poland and war in Europe began. Less than a year later, for the first time in America's history, there was peacetime conscription.

By early 1941, the US Congress had passed the Lend-Lease Act, providing the president with seven billion dollars to send weapons and aid to Britain and other countries, to combat the growing power of Hitler. This was a move to help without directly involving American troops. By the summer, the US Navy was escorting convoys west of Iceland and had authorization from the president to attack and sink enemy ships. It was Japan's sneak attack on the American Pacific Fleet at Pearl Harbor, Hawaii, early on the morning of 7 December 1941, that brought America into the war in an uprush of belated outrage and patriotism.

For Rod, the war presented not only a chance to serve his country, but to get away from the atmosphere of home and school. Forcing his mother to lie about his age – he is still acutely embarrassed that he had to twist her arm behind her back to make her sign – he enlisted in the US Navy, becoming a torpedo-man, first class, on a destroyer in the Pacific, involved in operations of the Third and Fifth Fleet. 'I loved the Navy. I was stupid enough to think I was being heroic,' he reflected later.

Although he had no idea what career he might follow, he gave his companions a foretaste of things to come by reciting Shakespeare one night while on watch. He hadn't noticed that his microphone was open until an officer on the bridge yelled, 'Get the hell off the line!'

Steiger persisted in his tannoyed turns, almost as though he had to be heard by as big an audience as possible: the need for fulfilment was there already. At that time Orson Welles was the sinister voice-over narrator of a popular radio series called *The Phantom Knows* – all about the secrets of the human heart, exposed for posterity in soapily operatic form.

On the ship's radio intercom Steiger constantly parodied the style and some of the substance of that programme. His stories were often comfortingly lewd for women-deprived men. They were a reminder of a world outside the grim rationale of military responsibilities and duties. Navels rather than naval.

Steiger used to end his nightly monologues with the words, 'The Phantom knows . . . and the Phantom says goodnight.'

Then one night came a blast on the all-ship microphone: 'And this is the captain on the bridge saying goodnight – and get the fuck off the air!'

But Steiger was back quite soon by popular request because the captain knew he had a morale-booster in these nightly tirades. Then the ship's padre butted in. He had enjoyed the parodies as much as anyone, and asked Rod to give a series of stand-up routines. 'They were the filthiest of all the jokes and stories I knew, but the chaplain loved them, rubbing his hands with joy. It really took their minds off the war,' Steiger proclaimed.

This lifting of the spirits was much needed. Not only was the ship engaged in combat, but – worse – there were the soldiers who were taken on board before battle. And after. 'When they came back they were far gone, too pitiful, most of them. When you've seen a man trying to dig fox-holes in steel decks you knew just how awful their lives had been made.'

Although Steiger saw enough action to turn him into a fervent pacifist, taking part in ten major engagements, one of his most frightening moments was being caught in a typhoon. 'It knocked the front off the battleship *Pennsylvania*. You certainly feel insignificant when you look up at a wave sixty feet above your head.' On 4 September 1945, the day after Japan formally surrendered to General MacArthur aboard the battleship *Missouri* in Tokyo

Bay, Rod left the Navy with a medical discharge: it was not a war wound, though, that necessitated the exit, but acne.

Or it might have been eczema – the medics were never quite sure. All Steiger knows is that he was allowed to wear a lighter shirt than other crew members, to ease the soreness of the rash that was his constant singlet of pain. 'It became a great joke to clap me on the back in supposed comradeship – and the blood would spurt through, so that there was a bloodied handmark on my vest. Great fun. It didn't hurt all that much, but it did get me noticed!'

Steiger also had his first sexual encounter while in the Navy, when his ship was harboured during its spell off-duty. North Fork, Virginia, was a place which found servicemen less than endearing. In the parks the signs read: 'Dogs and servicemen keep off the grass'.

Steiger went to a local dance-hall with some friends and spotted two girls, one blonde the other brunette, holding court with admiring swains. The girls were unresponding to each and every advance, enjoying their power, their disdain for the opposite sex. Steiger went over to chat up the blonde and was, equally, rebuffed. So he tried a ploy he had been working on for just such a contingency. 'Let me tell you a story,' he said. And he put a book of matches on the edge of the table, weighting it down with a glass. One match stuck out and Steiger lit it.

Then, timing it with the movement of the match, he said that there was a man in hospital who could not get an erection. The nurse said: 'Think about your wife.' The match sagged down. 'Think about your girlfriend,' urged the nurse. And the match straightened like an erection.

The girls laughed, especially the blonde, and Steiger took her off to seek a hotel. The town's attitude to servicemen was evident here as well. Servicemen could not get a room for the afternoon – it would have been too disgusting. So, master criminal he – or just desperate for sex – Steiger bought a small cardboard case and a fake wedding ring. Then he stormed into a hotel. 'My

31

wife and I are newly married. Where can we get a room? Where can we get a room? Look, do you want to see our marriage licence? I'm fighting for my country.' He reached into his inside pocket, but the receptionist was anxious to please such a noisy customer. Steiger and the blonde got the room and, in Steiger's words, 'We had one helluva time.'

Three days later he went to the urinal and began to tap-dance – 'it burned so much as I pissed. That's right, it was the clap. Thus do circumstances defeat master criminals!'

I said it sounded like a short story by Guy de Maupassant, with the beloved girl passing on the disease to the novice lover of lowly origins. He mused, 'You're right, it would make a neat parcel of a play. But, you know, I still feel saddened by the incident all these years afterwards. Losing my virginity should have been more important than that kind of demeaning disease.'

He is grateful to this day that he had a virginity to keep until that tender age. For he still remembers vividly an encounter with a paedophile when he was five years old.

There was a man, who lived near his mother's, who invited young Rodney in to look at a butterfly collection. Rod sat on the man's knee and the man began playing with the boy's genitals. 'This is why child-abuse is so monstrous. The child has no experience, he or she cannot comprehend what is happening to him. I *knew* it was wrong, deep-down, some instinct, but it was also very exciting. No child should ever have to be exposed to that kind of emotion.'

It only happened once. Next day he heard that the man had left the neighbourhood. Or been pushed from the neighbourhood? Steiger never knew. Fortunately, his first experience of sex had no lasting effects, and he developed a healthy desire for the opposite sex. Mind you, that could have its comic, subversive, side . . .

'As a young man you're so clever and sure of yourself: arrogant. I went with this woman who was a bit older than me. And I thought I would give her a good time, by being Casanova:

32

so I took my time, my good time, to do all the stroking and caressing, to make her ready for me.

'But she wasn't having any of that! She grabbed my hand as in a vice and almost pushed it up her vagina, with the rest of me following! Subtlety was not the name of this dame's game. It taught me a lesson, though, not to be over-confident.'

The adolescent had become a man, toughened by his experiences but hardly thinking of what lay ahead. He had no worries; it was enough to eat and sleep. He felt no real connection with the rest of the world; he was never to be quite sure whether that world had cut him off or if he had cut it off. Either way, it was mutual.

With nothing better to do, he left the Navy and returned to Newark to work in the Office of Dependants and Beneficiaries, taking home to his mother $27.50 a week. He was little more than a messenger, carting boxes stacked with cheques from one office to another and occasionally oiling the cheque-signing machines. It was a dreary existence.

His return home brought all those overwhelming emotions he had felt as a child to a head:

I don't have the temperament for a regular job. If I'd worked in one, I'd be the guy who, when he came into a bar, people would have said, 'Oh, Christ, here he comes again. Who's he going to pick a fight with tonight?' And one night someone would have slipped a knife between my ribs. I'd have been a miserable alcoholic. I was lucky. I belong to the luckiest minority: someone who can make a living at something he loves.

The influence of his unsettled upbringing and the lack of a father was to affect his future life. Like his father, he has found it difficult to settle, despite his desire for the sort of family life he never experienced as a child. 'I don't want my personal life ever to be one of agony, like John Barrymore's,' he once said. Yet

33

agony has marked his personal life, in a career punctuated by broken marriages, and terrible depressions.

The past contrived to impact upon his life. In 1968 he was filming the black comedy *No Way to Treat a Lady* in which he played a serial killer. Disguised as a hairdresser, he has murdered one of his victims and rings a detective to taunt him. As Steiger played the scene, he began to improvise, adding a W. C. Fields impersonation, ranting about degeneracy and debauchery and how much he had enjoyed killing. For a moment, he lost control. His voice took on a hysterical, menacing tone. He was shaken:

I was enjoying my hostility towards women. A certain piece of sickness in me happened to fit the situation. All of a sudden, under the guise of entertainment, came this psychological vomit. I scared myself. Something took over for about thirty seconds. It might have come out of the fact that for years I didn't like my mother at all, because she was an alcoholic. I had no use for her until I got older and realized she had a disease. Because that's what alcoholism is: a disease.

There was a concussed silence on the set after this rant, as though the crew had suddenly peered into an unexpected abyss. Steiger put the phone down and Jack Smight, the director, asked him, 'Do you want to do that again?'

'Never,' said Rod.

One of the best things Steiger remembers about his mother is that finally she managed to beat her alcohol craving. She was a member of Alcoholics Anonymous for the last eleven years of her life. When she was taken seriously ill, a few months before she died in 1967, Rod was sent for and told that she was dying; she would not breathe in the oxygen that was fed to her through a mask. She was sedated, too, which didn't help communication.

So Steiger sat down by her bed and yelled, 'Mom! You're acting like a cunt! You never were an actress, you could never sing, so why are you using this cheap way of attracting attention?' He ranted on like that, tears streaming down his cheeks and down the cheeks of everyone round the bedside.

But then she started to breathe, gulping back great breaths of oxygen. And her right hand came up to greet him.

'I knew that to make her angry was the only way to help her – even though I hated, just hated, doing it.'

By the time of his mother's death, Rod had been reconciled with her for many years. She had taken a vicarious pleasure in following his career and, with his stepfather Walter, watched his films more than once. She had kept scrapbooks detailing his work, even cutting out advertisements for his films in her local paper, where he was billed as 'North Jersey's Own Rod Steiger'. Rod's only regret was that she did not live to see him win an Oscar for his role as a Southern redneck sheriff in Norman Jewison's *In the Heat of the Night*. 'She would have died happy. She lived through me; she was a frustrated performer. But she went out knowing we loved each other; she's in a better place, waiting for me, as I'll wait for my son and daughter,' he says.

-2-

Every time you asked out an attractive woman you'd find she was always busy on a Thursday, which was the day I got paid and would have been able to afford a night out. I compared notes with the other guys and found that a drama group had been organized to which many of the girls belonged. The Office of Dependants and Beneficiaries had a cultural side. We came down on that drama group like vultures, but it wasn't culture that drew us.

This is Steiger's explanation for his initial interest in the theatre, equating art with an elemental need. Or is it as simple as that? I think that the theatre was a form of escapism for him that he perhaps only unconsciously realized. And, although sex may have been a prime motive, the backstage camaraderie also implied the idea of family which had always eluded him.

So he joined the drama group and was, before long, playing the lead in a raucous melodrama, *Curse You, Jack Dalton!*, well enough for the group's director, Rosa Palfrey, to suggest that he should study acting for a living. 'But actors were the golden people; I didn't understand. I only saw them on screen at the cinema after I'd washed the dishes and taken out the garbage and then my mother gave me ten cents for the local picture palace. I didn't even know you could actually study acting. I said I didn't have the money to study.'

Whatever can be said about the US government, it knew its responsibilities to its former military men. Under the GI Bill of

Rights Steiger found he was entitled to four years of schooling. The Bill of Rights guaranteed him an income of seventy-five dollars a month. He received another twenty-five dollars for his skin disability. It was an opportunity not to be missed; a chance for a decent exit from the life with his mother which was just as sour as it had been before he went away. 'I had feelings of loneliness, of hurt and of rage. And here was a profession that allowed me to get paid for doing what I enjoyed doing: emoting.'

For two years he studied acting at the New School for Social Research, where the German *émigré*, Erwin Piscator – 'a genius,' says Steiger – ran a dramatic workshop. The workshop was buzzing with life and energy and much else – another old boy, Walter Matthau, dubbed the place the Neurotic School for Sexual Research. Students worked from ten in the morning to late at night, taking classes in acting, movement, dance and voice, and listening to lectures on literature, art history and all aspects of culture.

Piscator had worked with Bertolt Brecht and influenced Joan Littlewood's Theatre Workshop in Britain and Living Newspaper productions in New York. He invited American actors and directors to work with his students. He also introduced the use of back projection and the turntable to the theatre.

Lee Strasberg, Stella Adler and Sanford Meisner were among those who welcomed the chance to have their dramatic theories explored while they explained. Leaving them way behind in their exploration were luminaries such as Steiger, Maureen Stapleton and Montgomery Clift. In the meantime, Steiger studied opera in a tenor voice that was to come in handy in *Oklahoma!* Rod was never going to be an opera singer. He had always sung at home with his mother on her good days and had developed a fine tenor voice with a big range. There was only one problem: he was tone deaf. He would change key halfway through an aria without knowing that he had done it. It was something he had to come to terms with.

'There is a sick child inside me that can never be satisfied,' Rod told me recently. 'I take for granted the good things that happen. It's sad, because I'm only learning now how thankful I should be. I had feelings of loneliness, of hurt and of rage. And the best thing that happened to me was that I got into a profession that allowed me to be paid for carrying on about it – a safe exorcism. It was a happy accident.'

Living the life of a mature student suited Steiger, this was what he wanted to do. In acting he found both a release and a satisfaction – a high of intense pleasure that was addictive and which was too often denied him in his personal life.

'I lived in a five-dollar room on West 81st Street with the john and the phone upstairs and water bugs as big as German submarines, which took about five whacks of a hammer instead of one to kill. They were amazing things. They made Sherman tanks look like sissies.'

So, of course, did some of the egos with which Steiger was to become involved, as he discovered what the Method School of Acting entailed – especially as the Actors' Studio was to be his preferred goal in dramatic tuition.

It was not easy to join the Actors' Studio, though once in you were a member for life. The normal method of entry was by audition: if you failed, you could come back another year. Some determined actors auditioned twelve or thirteen times before they were accepted. Rod was luckier. He did not audition at all.

It happened that Daniel Mann, Rod's teacher at the American Theatre Wing, had been asked by his friend Elia Kazan to help out at the Actors' Studio while Kazan was busy directing a Broadway play. Rod had been pleased that he'd emerged with credit from one of Mann's tougher assignments: to do a quarrel scene from Thomas Wolfe's novel *The Web and the Rock*, without leaving out a word of the original. At the end of the summer term, Mann invited a couple of students to come to work at the Actors' Studio. To Rod, he said nothing.

Bitterly disappointed, Steiger walked out of the class to make his way home, feeling very sorry for himself – and there is nobody who can look as hangdog as Steiger when he puts his mind to it. 'My head was almost between my legs,' he remembered. Ahead of him, he could see Mann striding along the pavement. Suddenly, Mann turned round and yelled at him, 'Hey, Rod! Rod! I'll see you at the Actors' Studio in the fall!'

Rod was ecstatic: 'My heart blossomed. I was the happiest little kid that ever lived on the block.'

Although Rod feels he no longer uses the Method, there is no doubt that it was a kick-start to his talent as it was to so many others. Even today, when the Method is established as the predominant style of American acting, when the most admired actors, such as Robert De Niro, Al Pacino and Dustin Hoffman, are among its adherents, it remains controversial, not least in the way De Niro so often follows Steiger in his approach, even to his vocal mechanisms and body language.

Steiger eschews the description 'Method' now, but recognizes the way it liberated the actor – to be emotional without being condemned. 'The word was very much a press thing. But it was a wonderful tool. Why, it even allowed men to cry.'

British actors, trained in classical theatre with its emphasis on immaculate diction, still regard it with suspicion, as do many of the survivors of the generation of Hollywood actors who came to film before the 1950s. In 1996, Mickey Rooney, while giving a workshop in Scotland, was still insisting that Marlon Brando became a star only when he abandoned the methods of the Method.

One of its first American adherents, the theatre and film director Harold Clurman, defined the Method as 'teaching the actor to put the whole gamut of his physical and emotional being into the service of the dramatist's meaning'.

It had its origins in the work of the Russian director Konstantin Stanislavsky at the Moscow Arts Theatre in the 1890s and early 1900s. He systematized the way actors could prepare themselves for interpreting plays, detailing it in three books. But as Clurman pointed out, 'Every teacher of the Method lends it the quality of his own mind and disposition. There is no longer an "orthodox" Method, only a group of teachers (most of them trained in America) whose lessons derive from, but are not limited to, the Stanislavsky sources.'

The most simplistic way to work with the idea is to relate some of the dramatist's emotions to your own. This has led the way to some extraordinary explosions of passion or some laughable damp squibs. Anti-Methodists conjured jokes to defuse the intensity of approach. Director to ingenue: 'You've just been dreadfully raped by a gang. How do you tell your parents?' Ingenue: 'Mummy, I'm engaged.' Or the suggestion to that same ingenue: 'Don't just do something; stand there.'

The Method's great influence on Rod's generation of actors was due mainly to the formidable, forceful personality of Lee Strasberg at the Actors' Studio. This had been started in October 1947, in a former Union Methodist Church on New York's West 48th Street, by Elia Kazan and his friend, director Robert Lewis. It had been set up as a free training school, open to all with the necessary talent.

Two months later, in December, Kazan directed Marlon Brando on Broadway in Tennessee Williams' *A Streetcar Named Desire*, a performance that in its revolutionary impact cast a lustre over his newly founded school. The Studio also owed some of its early prestige to its links with the Group Theatre, which had been set up in 1929 by Clurman, Cheryl Crawford and Strasberg, and where Kazan had begun as an actor. Crawford became the Studio's administrator and when Lewis left after its first year, an initially reluctant Strasberg was persuaded to replace him.

Austrian-born, Strasberg was introspective and dictatorial, liked and hated in equal measure. After his death in 1982, members of the Actors' Studio, interviewed by Foster Hirsch for a history of Method acting, compared him to God, Jesus,

Buddha, Moses, the Pope, Oedipus, Pontius Pilate, Rasputin and Hitler. His detractors saw him as a destructive force, one who insisted that his pupils copy his monotonous and often mumbling speech. Marlon Brando, the actor who came to epitomize the Method, has said that he had little respect for Strasberg, and credits another teacher, Stella Adler, who was married to Harold Clurman, with changing the style of American acting in the fifties and sixties.

Strasberg ruled with a Stalinist glare and temper, which is not the best way to control actors who might sound tough, but also be very vulnerable, like Steiger. But Steiger used the principle of Method well enough in his own work, even helping others. A Jewish colleague was supposed to be mightily enraged, but came across as merely exhibiting a tantrum. Steiger took him out to lunch, talking to him about newsreels of the concentration camps. How did he feel about Hitler? 'I could kill him!' Steiger suggested he used that venom on stage and the man did so – so forcefully that Steiger admits the hair stood up on the back of his neck.

To his admirers, Strasberg was a guru whose every word was law. Shelley Winters, when she was acting opposite Rod in the film *The Big Knife*, was happy to fly from Hollywood to New York just to seek his advice when she was having trouble with her role as a blackmailing hooker. He told her to act the girl's courage – 'just be afraid of the furniture, as if it could come to life and hurt you.' She thought his advice was inspired. 'Lee had helped me be funny and brave and at the same time communicate "nameless dread".'

She said about those early days, 'We were dedicated to the idea of great theatre. We all thought we would do Shakespeare plays and marry each other.'

Kazan had deliberately chosen Lewis over Strasberg when he began the Studio because Lewis' teaching had qualities of simplicity, clarity and humour, all of which he felt Strasberg's methods lacked. Some felt Strasberg always exhibited the traits

41

he had shown in the first years of the Group Theatre. Kazan explained, 'Lee was God almighty, he was always right, only he could tell if an actor had it – the real thing of quality – or not. To win Lee's favour and the reassurance it would convey was everyone's goal . . . There was little joy in Lee's work.'

But Kazan's final verdict on Strasberg's reign at the Actors' Studio was: 'Over the years, respect became hero worship, idolatry.'

That respect is evident in the words of James Dean, when he passed his audition at the age of twenty-one. He wrote in triumph to his aunt and uncle, 'I am very proud to announce that I am a member of The Actors' Studio. The greatest school of the theatre . . . It is the best thing that can happen to an actor.'

Ego, though, had something to do with it. Steiger told me:

I knew Jimmy Dean pretty well; not as close as some people, but I was one of the few people he seemed to have some respect for. I remember getting a phone call when he was making *Giant*. And he said, could I come out to Warner Brothers, as he was having trouble with the director, George Stevens – 'he doesn't know what he's doing'. So I said, 'I don't know about that, but he is a very talented film director who can put a film together as good as anybody, or better. So is it a personality thing?' There are, of course, quite a few directors who don't know how to handle actors, but I didn't think Stevens would be one of them.

Anyway, I met Jimmy in the commissary at Warner Brothers and he ordered a steak and he was telling me he was having trouble, so I said, 'Well, whatever, don't argue with the man in front of people – they depend on him for their livelihood – don't do that to big egos – don't do that to anyone.'

So I suggested that what he do is say to him, 'You gave me an idea to do the scene' and then say, 'How was that?' Nine out of ten times it'll work and he'll be happy to take the credit. You get to do it your way and they think it's their way and everyone's happy. But don't forget: too much discussion can be the death of art.

Meanwhile, Jimmy's eaten three-quarters of the steak and he suddenly tells the waitress that he doesn't like the steak – she should take it back. She pointed out that he had nearly eaten it all. And he said, 'Look, this is Hollywood, baby! TAKE IT BACK . . .' And you know I felt this chill inside me, because I figured, my God! that this was the first sign of a person being so drenched in their own ego that it would lead to their destruction. There is a terrible phrase called 'Going Hollywood'. I think that's what happened to Jimmy. You know Jimmy killed himself in his car crash, but he always was fascinated by the idea of death. He once gave me his most precious book, Ernest Hemingway's *Death in the Afternoon*, which is about bull-fighting as a fine art – implicitly a death wish.

Jimmy Dean was surrounded by a lot of people whom I called not the Gay People, but the Grey People: weird groups of people, strange sexual practices. You have to remember that we're animals and titillation and our senses are always more powerful than our intellects. And actors deal with feelings all the time. You can get good feelings out of that and you can get dreadful feelings. Jimmy Dean died too young, but just right for his legend, if that's what it is. And he was young enough to avoid the terrible, flagellatory death of Montgomery Clift.

The principles of the Method could not mask Steiger's innate nature. But the technique came in for its own kind of retaliation from people who may have felt threatened by it. It was, after all, an acting weapon of the defiant young. Piscator thought the Method was 'sugared realism, not real realism'. When Charles Laughton was directing *Major Barbara* on Broadway in the mid-fifties he told Eli Wallach, 'I don't want any of that Stanislavsky shit from you.' Paul Henreid, an elegant actor and director who had been trained in Austria and began as a member of Max Reinhardt's company, approved of the Method 'as Kazan and Stella Adler taught it'. But he added, 'The Strasberg school leaves me cold. I never felt Lee Strasberg could act, and I fail to see how someone who can't act can teach acting.'

Laurence Olivier sat in on one of Strasberg's classes and thought he spoke 'a lot of hot air, sprinkled with clichés'. Olivier's advice to actors was, 'By all means have Stanislavsky with you in your study or your limousine or wherever you are three hours before the scene, but don't bring him on to the film set, where the schedule is tight and the time is ripe for fizzing action to carry along the actors.' Or, as he put it rather more succinctly, 'Work on a building site rather than go to a "Method Studio".' His views were coloured by his experience of working with Marilyn Monroe on the film *The Prince and the Showgirl*, in which he felt her natural talent had been suppressed by the rigmarole of the Method, and the intimidating presence of Mrs Strasberg. Indeed, I had met Marilyn at the time and had noted her nervous reliance on her mentor.

In the late fifties, Noël Coward spent a morning at the Actors' Studio – 'far more hilarious than I had ever imagined it to be' – and listened to Strasberg's 'long dissertation on the art of acting, most of which was pretentious balls'. He watched a scene from *Mourning Becomes Electra* and judged:

Never have I seen such affected, downright inept acting. When they had finished, they settled down to explain themselves and be talked to by God, and I suddenly got enraged and went out. Cathleen [Nesbitt] stayed, however, and telephoned me later. Apparently one student had had the temerity to criticize the inaudibility, whereupon Lee Strasberg flew at him and said audibility didn't matter a good Goddamn and it was the moment of truth that counted! It is this monumental nonsense which is spreading like a disease over the American theatre. What is so maddening is that out of it have emerged some good actors, but my guess is talent, true talent, can survive anything.

Coward echoed Olivier's views on Marilyn Monroe. When she died of an overdose in 1962, he wrote in his diary:

Poor silly creature. I am convinced that what brought her to that final foolish gesture was a steady diet of intellectual pretentiousness pumped into her over the years by Arthur Miller and 'The Method' . . . I am sure that all the idiocies of her last few years, always being late on the set, etc., plus over-publicity and too many theoretical discussions about acting, were the result of all this constant analysis of every line in every part she had to play, and a desperate longing to be 'intellectual' without the brain to achieve it.

The hostile attitude of the pre-Method generation is best summed up by the reaction of Jackie Coogan, at a time when Charlie Chaplin's co-star from *The Kid* had grown up to become a character actor. In the days of live television, Coogan had problems when rehearsing a play with a Method actor, who never looked at him but kept staring at his shoes, caught in the throes of some deep emotion. Coogan, like most actors, wanted eye contact with his fellow player. The Method actor refused, saying it would spoil his concentration on his own role. When they came to shoot the play live, the actor, as usual, looked down at his shoes. As director Richard Fleischer tells the story, 'This time, though, Coogan's shoes came into his field of vision. On one shoe he had written the word "Fuck" and on the other "You".'

Eye-contact, though, was one of the most important things for Steiger. Years later, when he made a British TV thriller with Anthony Perkins, he lamented that Perkins – who had become a superstar via Hitchcock's *Psycho* – was almost mental about meeting Steiger's gaze. 'That's because he was doped up most of the time. It was very aggravating; you couldn't get a fix on the guy or his character. He had already had his fix of whatever he was on.'

The atmosphere at the Actors' Studio from the 1950s on tended to be reverential. 'Opinions were offered fearfully,' said Kazan. 'Suppose Lee didn't agree? Suppose he took offence? We'd all been made aware of his temper. Sometimes responses were offered in a tremulous voice. An actor might preface his statement with: "As you said last time, Lee", or "Like you always say, Lee", followed by an observation he had reason to believe Lee would agree with. I'm not sure Lee liked this crawling, but he didn't stop it.'

Tony Curtis recalls being surprised when, as a young actor, he attended a lecture there and found that he was being used as an example of how bad film acting was:

I was really pissed off, but I went back one more time to watch. Maybe I was missing something. I wasn't. That whole Strasberg school was created by the idiosyncrasies and genius of one man, Marlon Brando. From him, not Strasberg, came the likes of James Dean and Paul Newman and Monty Clift and John Cassavetes. It was a mind fuck: Go off in your head somewhere to find some other reality for what you were doing, regardless of what the script intended.

The technique was more properly called Affective Memory and was valued by Rod and other Actors' Studio alumni. Strasberg once explained, 'Using Affective Memory, which the great actors used unconsciously, makes it possible for us to join in the great tradition of acting. When Kean in *Hamlet* picked up the skull of Yorick, he cried, because he said he always thought of his uncle.'

Shelley Winters, who had attended the Actors' Studio while playing in *Oklahoma!* on Broadway, said that Strasberg:

taught me how to do an Affective Memory exercise, for which I must find a powerful traumatic experience in my own life, remember the sensory details of that moment and, with another section of my mind, recall them as I acted. It's what makes the playwright's words come out of your own experience. When I finally learned to use this correctly, it became the most powerful tool I ever used in acting.'

Steiger gave an example of it in action when he was directing his own translation of Frank Wedekind's *The Tenor* at the Studio. Rod himself played an opera singer who is brought a new work by a composer and tells the man that anything he sings will be successful so that there is no need to try to be original. The composer replies, 'Don't ever talk to me like that! I'm an artist!'

Steiger felt that the actor could do better with the line and took him to lunch. That's when he suggested he use his violent feelings about Hitler. In similar fashion, Kazan used to find out as much as possible about an actor's personal life and would use what he knew in rehearsals to get the performance he wanted from his actors.

Steiger found it a helpful technique. When he wanted to express his hatred of somebody, he would say to himself, 'He's the person who killed Harry Baur!' Rod had great admiration for the beefy French actor who, like him, had played Rasputin. Baur, who had begun his career on stage in 1904 at the age of twenty-three, had been an outstanding presence in thirties films. Following the detention of his Jewish wife, he had been arrested by the Nazis in 1943 as an Allied agent, and tortured by the Gestapo, dying just after he had been released from prison. 'I keep the emotion fresh by thinking this guy not only killed Baur, he put lighted straws under his fingernails first.'

Every actor, Rod felt, had to adapt the technique to suit themselves. 'Every distinctive artist remains an individual. Instead of somehow submitting himself to the character, he has to find the nearest way of personally identifying with him.'

47

With some adherents of the Method, acting became almost a branch of therapy and many who spent time at the Actors' Studio, including Brando and Steiger, were to spend time on psychiatrists' couches as well. Their performances were sometimes over-emotional. As Robert Lewis put it, 'Crying, after all, is not the sole object of acting. If it were, my old Aunt Minnie would be Duse.'

Critic Roger Ebert noted that, unlike other Method actors, Steiger lacked mannerisms. 'When he gets a character worth playing with, he creates it new from the bottom up, out of whole cloth. I don't know how he does it. It's almost as if he gets inside the skin of the guy he's playing and starts being that person for a while.'

Rod, indeed, thought acting was like analysis, since it required the ability to understand and dissect a character. But he went further, believing that some actors had established themselves as personalities because of 'personal neuroses that have been made commercial'.

Clurman was perceptive on the dangers of a reliance on Affective Memory: 'Those with whom it agrees not only use it but often become consumed by it. With the immature and more credulous actor it may even develop into an emotional self-indulgence, or in other cases into a sort of private therapy. The actor being the ordinary neurotic man suffering all sorts of repressions and anxieties seizes upon the revelation of himself – supplied by the recollection of his past – as a purifying agent. Through it, he often imagines he will not only become a better actor, but a better person. It makes him feel that because of it he is no longer a mere performer but something like a redeemed human being and an artist.'

Brando and his devoted admirer, James Dean, were soon to give Method actors a not entirely complimentary image in the tabloid press, one that the Hollywood gossip columnist Louella Parsons defined as 'the professionally unwashed, unmannered, unconventional'. Steiger is not forgiving. '*They* will continue to be remembered worldwide and for decades to come. Miss Parsons – washed, perfumed and buried – is remembered only in showbiz.'

More seriously, there were critics who felt that the Method was an essentially theatrical approach to acting, often dependent not so much on individual talent, as drawing on effects that had worked well in the past. The *New Yorker*'s Pauline Kael felt, for instance, that when Rod gave a soundless scream while crouching over the dead body of a youth in *The Pawnbroker*, audiences with good memories filled the silence by thinking, 'Ah yes, that must be the famous Berliner Ensemble scream. I've heard of it but I've not heard it before.' Rod will tell you that the inspiration for that moment came from seeing Picasso's *Guernica* with its keening women, heads back, mouths open, 'the loudest scream I ever heard'. Then again, I've heard Steiger compare that scream to artist Francis Bacon's picture series of Screaming Popes, which were taken from Eisenstein's *Battleship Potemkin* and the Odessa Steps sequence. You pays your money and you takes your choice.

Kazan, too, grew to dislike the Studio's acting style, writing, 'I would prefer more humour and verve and less self-indulgence, self-pity, and self-awareness. I detest emotional striptease.' It was typical of Kazan that he should double back on himself as he did so, politically, in Hollywood. Perhaps he consoled himself with the thought that it was a U-turn, but it was a left-wing U-turn.

Perhaps the last word on the subject of the Method belongs to Steiger. 'Actors may be the purest of all artists, because we attempt to reach others, and give something to them through ourselves only. The actor has no instrument but himself.

'You can love beautifully in the fantasy of your art even when you can hardly live in the reality of your own life. An actor's highest moments come when his instincts and his intellect meet and they together communicate something to another person.

'I do believe the actor can, through acting, exchange his

discoveries about himself with his fellow man. Any actor who doesn't attempt to communicate truthfully with others ceases to exist as a creative artist. If any actor has one inspired moment in a performance, he can be called good; more than one and he's great. If he has none, he'll bore himself – and the public – to death.

'To me Method acting is anything that gets you involved personally in the part, so that you can communicate in human terms with an audience. Despite all the obstacles and bad-mouthing, the American actor changed the acting of the world. It started with an actor named Montgomery Clift, so do not put us or any artist down for not having the ability to be consistently great.'

It was to be Brando, Dean and Clift who were to epitomize the new breed of stars in the public mind – slouching masculine figures (though two at least, unknown to their many female fans, were homosexual, and Clift later denounced Strasberg as a charlatan), rebels with whom adolescent youths could identify. Rod missed out, partly through his looks. He lacked the androgynous grace of Dean and Clift and the Roman profile of Brando. He also tended to play roles older than himself. In *On the Waterfront*, he is Brando's older brother, although in reality Brando was born the year before Rod. His appeal, you could say, was more adult. Rod Steiger was never going to be a teenager's heart throb. But the pulse of his art was to be a much more complex beat. Of all of those following Lee Strasberg, he marched to a different drum. His own nature.

– 3 –

R od sought a settled way of life, but it tended to elude him. He believed that, first of all, a man had to provide for himself and his family. 'You've got to bring food into the house before you can start talking about ideals.' When he first began to earn real money as an actor, he bought a home on the Pacific Ocean at Malibu. He has managed to hold on to it despite divorces, periods of living abroad, forest fires and deep depressions. It has housed his most treasured possessions, including an engraving by Van Gogh and, framed near it, a leaf Rod had picked from Van Gogh's grave. 'I have tried to maintain my self-respect in a house with good food, and still hold on to the luxury of my naïve ideals,' he says.

In the beginning, as a struggling young actor in New York, there was little luxury. His mother would send him food parcels to supplement his meagre meals. They now had a distanced, working relationship.

Life improved in 1952, when he met Sally Gracie, a young red-haired actress who had also come to New York to make a career for herself in the theatre. They were soon attracted to one another and married. 'Rod was more set up for entertaining than most of us,' remembered actress Carroll Baker, who made her name as the original Baby Doll. She had gone to Rod's apartment with a future husband, Jack Garfein, a young director who worked at the Actors' Studio, for weekly play readings. Sally would make the coffee and they would sit around the kitchen table with their scripts. It was often Ibsen, whose plays

Steiger loved, having staged a workshop production of *Peer Gynt*.

But the marriage was marked by disagreements. Rod was ambitious, and found it hard to concentrate on anything else. The romance soured, though the couple tried, over fourteen months, to salvage the relationship, even after they were divorced. Rod admitted, 'I couldn't handle my career and marriage.' It's a clichéd excuse, but none the less valid; the tunnel-vision necessary in any actor's life can admit few diversions.

There were several separations during their time together. From early on, Rod had sought, reluctantly, help from a psychoanalyst. At first he resisted the treatment, until his analyst told him that he should only give up if he felt that increasing his self-knowledge was damaging him. His analysis, he realized, was a learning experience. 'It is a trained mind teaching another human being how he can use himself better, how he can function better. And isn't that what we all want to do?' he reflected. Well, you do if you want to be a better actor; after all, being concerned with the Method, you work with what you've got – or can get. Useful material, there: material which Steiger was to use later, in 1961, when he played a psychiatrist, Dr Edmund McNally.

One late attempt to get together again came in 1956, when Rod moved to London to begin preparations for his first British film, *Across the Bridge*. Sally flew to London to meet him and they went to spend some time together in Italy. Rod told reporters that they wanted to start a family. 'I'm hoping it will make us both happier human beings,' he said. But the attempt failed, and it was not for another two years that he experienced the happiness, however brief, of another marriage.

His next two marriages followed the same pattern:

Like most people, I believe I confused sex with love, the physical satisfaction with the depth of the love I might think I was entertaining. I always remember in my marriages, the sexual thing would start great and when it levelled off and started to take its position so you weren't making love every night, I'd begin to confuse that with the loss of romance, with the loss of love. And I didn't like the person any more. And then you'd get to the quiet periods, and a terrible stiffened politeness, maintaining the marriage in a papier mâché form. The periods of silence would get longer. Then the frozen feelings in the stomach as the car turns towards the house, and your instincts don't want to go in there any more, a fear or an anger takes over. That happened to me in every one of my marriages. I didn't know then that love was a lot of work. Hard work.

In January 1959 during a lull in his screen career Rod, seeking fresh challenges, returned to the Broadway stage because he believed that the roots of creative acting were in the theatre. He played an outlaw in *Rashomon*, dramatized by Fay and Michael Kanin from stories by Ryunosuke Akutagawa that had been the basis of Akira Kurosawa's masterpiece, a film that more than any other had made the world aware of the quality of Japanese cinema.

Among the good-luck telegrams sent to Rod on his opening night was one from Sally, DEAR DARLING ROLL FOR THE GREEN LOVE. But by then Rod was in love with another woman, his co-star Claire Bloom, an actress who came from a different culture to his own. Born into a middle-class family in London, she had been an actress from the age of fifteen, studied at the Guildhall School of Music and Drama and before long, was being hailed as a great new star. She first played Ophelia to both Paul Scofield's and Robert Helpmann's Hamlets at Stratford-upon-Avon and was then chosen by Charles Chaplin to star opposite him in *Limelight*. This role catapulted her to international fame; a pensive photograph of her appeared on the cover of *Time* magazine above the caption, 'A star is born'. When *Limelight* opened in London in 1952, Claire was getting ecstatic reviews for her performance as Juliet at London's Old Vic.

Coolly elegant in a very English way, she also had a habit of falling in love with her leading men. She'd had affairs with Richard Burton (she'd been Ophelia to his Hamlet at the Old Vic), and Yul Brynner, with whom she had starred in *The Buccaneer*. Later in her career, in 1972, George Cukor cast her, against screen type, as a nymphomaniac in *The Chapman Report*, which at the time attracted controversy as the sexiest mainstream movie ever made. Said Cukor, 'Claire is not a nice Nellie. She has no inhibitions, and she is not as cold as some people say.'

Steiger had thought her aloof when they first met, for she had a natural shyness. She had been surprised at how young he was. Claire was not expecting to be attracted to Rod. She expected him to be too tough and too prosaic to appeal to her; instead she found that beneath the tough-guy manner he was 'sensitive, sentimental, kind, even if, like many actors, self-involved'.

Despite their closeness during the run, they denied plans for marriage. 'I don't see how anyone can deny being interested in a lovely woman, but nobody's getting married,' said Rod. But when the play ended, Claire moved into Rod's apartment in Greenwich Village. Then they went on holiday together to Naples and Sicily. When they returned, she discovered she was pregnant. Rod proposed, and in September they were married in the Malibu sheriff's office, near Rod's beloved beach house. 'If our priorities were more need than passion,' Claire wrote in her recent autobiography, 'our relationship gave us many years of supportive family happiness.'

Had she not been pregnant, she would not have married, and the affection she came to feel for Rod was not enough to keep them together for ever. But both were overjoyed by the birth of their daughter on 13 February 1960, an event that Claire regards as the most triumphant experience of her life. Says Rod,

'My daughter, Anna Justine, conceived in love, was the first real commitment I ever had in my life.' They named her Anna after Anna Karenina and Justine after the heroine of Lawrence Durrell's novel of the same name, which was then Claire's favourite. Two months after the birth, Claire was back at work, filming in Berlin with Curt Jurgens.

The London journalist (and later novelist) Thomas Wiseman asked the couple who would make the sacrifices in case of career conflicts. 'I would,' said Claire. 'Anyway, I shall have my child to look after.' Wiseman found that 'sweetness and tranquillity pervades all. The atmosphere is fraught with genteel bliss.'

Claire had told reporters that she would take at least a year off acting after the baby arrived and would not be employing a nanny. (In fact, from the age of three months until she was thirteen, her daughter had a Swiss nurse, Helene, as a constant companion.) A year after the marriage, Rod was telling showbusiness journalist Kenneth Passingham:

She is all I wanted in a woman. And we don't intend to take any risks by being separated. You know what it is in this business. Besides, you cannot play around with a child's emotional welfare.

Maybe our marriage is better than most because we were both established when we met. There is no ambitious friction – we don't have to compete. That would be fatal.

But, for two actors – and one happier when on stage – separations from each other were inevitable. And Rod, nicknamed 'The Weeper' in Hollywood for his ability to show emotions, had a very different approach from Claire, who once said, 'I am allergic to any kind of emotion.'

Her attitude to the marriage was to change from this early euphoria. She began to regret that her career no longer came first. In *Limelight and After*, the first volume of her autobiography, she wrote that getting married in 1959 was 'one of the great pivotal performances and, for an actress's career, one of the worst. Your career stops. For the next ten years everything I did was a compromise between looking after my child and working. The work came second.'

Steiger loved the peace and isolation that Malibu provided. Claire hated it, finding it dull and boring. She disliked the Hollywood gossip and missed the excitements and culture of big city life and her friends. So work she did, in films and plays in California or London, depending where the work was, while Anna studied at the Lycée Français. Claire, trained in English stagecraft and a professional from the age of fifteen, was not sympathetic to the Method approach to acting, though she admitted learning something valuable from Rod: boldness. She felt that had more to do with his temperament than with his training.

'I've been told that Method acting is an enormous exposure of what you are – accent on enormous and you,' she wrote. 'Yet, when one meets in the flesh the you who's been exposing himself enormously, one often finds that there's no one there, no self at all.'

Steiger comments: 'Poor Claire! She always had to live through other people. I don't think she knew who she really was.'

Rod was to make two films with Claire. They had hoped to work together more, but the problem was finding scripts which provided them with equal parts. As a result, their work often separated them. 'I wouldn't think of asking my wife to give up her career,' Rod said, while Claire was making *The Spy Who Came in from the Cold*. 'You can't tell another person, "Don't do this", because you will have the person blaming you in ten years' time, saying, "You stopped me".' He felt that they were both often selfish, but each, as a creative person, understood the need of the other to be so. 'The excitement of doing a new part temporarily blinds you to the rest of the world. I'm the dullest of husbands when I fall in love with a role.'

Certainly he and Claire sparked when they were together, as my wife and I discovered when they came to dinner. Both of them presented entertaining arguments for their styles of acting. Nothing dull about that. Steiger would give a cut-glass rendition of the way he thought RADA students spoke; Claire took on a Method semblance at its most messy, with an 'uh' and an 'oh' of the kind Brando had become notorious for. It was a tricky sort of conflict which, had it not been conducted in terms of banter, would have seemed lethally unpleasant. Thinking back, though, perhaps it was; we just hadn't realized it at the time. Nor had they, I think.

When they did find work together, the scripts may have given them equal parts, but they were not the best choices. The first, *The Illustrated Man*, from Ray Bradbury's short-story collection, was interesting rather than successful. They followed it with *Three Into Two Won't Go*, which was one of theatre director Peter Hall's failed attempts at film. Hall had been looking forward to working with Rod; he was aware of his reputation for improvisation during filming and hoped for an exciting collaboration. 'One must leave well alone,' he said before filming began. But he found the actual experience a complete nightmare and felt that he was never able to exercise any control over Rod. (Hall confided in his diaries, 'Considerable things were expected of me, and because I was learning the trade, they didn't happen.')

Ray Bradbury, who is an old friend of mine from the days – as he put it – before he *was* Ray Bradbury, says:

Rod was very good in it, but it wasn't a good film. There had been a guy going round with a plagiarized version of the idea, but I cleared him off. And I used to keep contact with it by going down to the film set and I saw Rod being tattooed – an arduous, painful process. But the script was terrible, because they'd started in the wrong place and taken the guts out of it. Rod rang me to say that he thought the script was awful as well and he was re-writing bits and pieces. But, whatever

57

he says, he's not a writer and that's why it didn't work.

Actors! Rod is very combative. I remember when he and his then wife came to dinner and I had invited an actor called Monte Markham and Rod said, 'Monte Markham? What kind of name is THAT?' And I could almost hear Markham's hair bristle! My wife, Maggie, had seated the two of them side by side for dinner. Well, after a while, I had to part them and sit between them, because they just wouldn't mix. Actors!

Steiger enjoyed *Three Into Two Won't Go* more, even adding some lines to the script to sum up how he felt about its unhappily married couple. 'What the hell are we chewing at each other for? We gave it twelve years. It didn't work, but we never admitted it until now. That's our crime. That we pretended.' It was a line that echoed what was fast becoming their real-life relationship.

Claire Bloom remembered that Rod had to play a drunk scene in the film to her, playing his wife, and Peggy Ashcroft, playing his mother-in-law. He was, she thought, appalling.

The English contingent, Peggy and I and the director Peter Hall, were dumbstruck. He'd been all over the place, no control, no sense, just the spewing out of the scene. Peter Hall said to me, 'Can you speak to him?' I said, 'I have nothing to do with him as an actor. I'm here to play my part and he's here to play his part and I wouldn't dream of it.' And he said, 'But what about *that*?' I said, 'Well, I've never seen anything so terrible in my life.' So we took it again and he controlled it somewhat, and then we did a third take, and on the fourth he was wonderful.

One of the unexpected benefits of being married to Claire Bloom was an introduction to Charles Chaplin. Chaplin was, of course, one of the greatest names in cinema: actor, clown, director, writer, producer and composer. He had done all his best work in Hollywood, which – during the monstrous phase of the Un-

American Activities Committee – branded him a commie, a left-winger, an agitator.

He was a man who had dragged himself up by his own bootstraps. Born during the reign of Queen Victoria, he was nearer to the art of Charles Dickens than of today's world, to which he found it difficult to adjust. Claire had co-starred with him in his *Limelight*, the story of a fading music-hall comedy star. She had found favour with the great man, so Steiger accompanied her to visit Chaplin in his retreat in Switzerland.

Steiger admired Chaplin to the point of adoration, not just because of the man's vast talents but because he identified with Chaplin's slum origins that he too had fought against. Hard-timers recognize each other.

But at first Chaplin only saw him as Claire's companion, not as an individual. Steiger, when he tells of the visit, puts on the staccato, high-pitched English accent that was Chaplin's towards the end of his life. Recognition only really began at the end of the day when, after a walking tour, he and Chaplin were left alone at the dinner-table and Chaplin asked if Steiger had ever played Hamlet.

'No, I haven't!'

'No? Good God, man, why not?'

Steiger pointed out that he didn't think he was the right physical type. And also, 'I feel that Hamlet has been twisted out of shape during the years since he was created. I don't think he was the way Mr Shakespeare created him.'

There was a silence as Chaplin reflected on this interpretation. Then he was up and walking rapidly round the room. 'By God, you're right. You're right. Over the years he would be conditioned, he would be altered. He would be no longer "pure".'

After that he asked Steiger to call him Charles, although Steiger thought that was too presumptuous. But he revealed things about himself that had been secret, such as the fact that President Kennedy had asked the exiled Chaplin to come back to America three times. 'But I was too hurt.'

59

There were examples of how the rich can really live – such as driving fifty-seven miles to a farm to buy half a pint of cream for some strawberries. 'Look at that – that's real cream!' said Chaplin. 'You can stand your spoon up in it.'

Steiger asked if they could see a Chaplin film, but Chaplin professed not to hear him. Steiger especially wanted to see *Monsieur Verdoux*, but Oona, Chaplin's wife, said, 'You've come during the wrong cycle. Now he thinks all his films are crap. But in a couple of months he'll do a reassessment and we'll watch them all the way through.'

Then one day Chaplin said, 'We will see a film.' Overjoyed, Steiger accompanied Claire into the preview theatre. But it was a film called *Tadpole*. And it was about a small boy in a suit of armour, whose sword breaks. Was that all? 'Yes, that was one of my sons at his birthday party. I called him Tadpole.'

Another day Steiger got up early, but not as early as Chaplin. Steiger tip-toed towards the swimming pool, past Chaplin, elegantly dressed in a cravat and blazer, who was already dictating to a secretary. 'What ARE you doing?' he shouted at Steiger.

Steiger said, 'I didn't want to disturb you. I was going to have a swim.'

'Nonsense. You're not disturbing me. I was just totting up my communistic shares in the big American corporations. They're worth quite a bit.' Steiger says, 'Now I knew what Charles Chaplin's politics were.'

Steiger says that when he likes or admires somebody he teases them – sometimes too much. He did that with Chaplin, who seemed to enjoy it. 'I noticed that, at dinner, he would check what everyone else was having. It's a habit you get from a poverty-stricken childhood. So I said, as we started a meal, "Sir, I am having two lamb chops. I thought you would like to know."' And took two chops from the salver handed to him by the butler.

Chaplin twinkled, 'Good God, man, you can have as many

60

chops as you like – thirty, forty. Kind of you to let me know, though.'

Marlon Brando, who worked with Chaplin on *The Countess From Hong Kong*, thought it was hateful the way he treated his sons. When Steiger left, Oona said, 'Did Charles call you "my boy"?' Steiger said he had. Oona looked wistful. 'That's more than he ever has done for his sons.'

But by this time the marriage of Claire and Steiger was falling apart. Claire had noticed that actresses either married weak and often dull men who were happy to take a subsidiary role, or demanding and interesting men with a life of their own. Neither was satisfactory. She also was aware that having children took its toll; many actresses were unable to return and sustain a career after time away from the stage. She felt that what was most herself would die if the actress within her died.

What she was also to discover, after she and Rod divorced, was that Anna resented her mother going off to work, while not minding the fact that Rod did the same. 'Something died along the way,' said Rod. 'I'll take sixty per cent blame for the break.'

Rod was upset not only by the divorce, but the speed with which she married again, to Broadway producer Hillard Elkins whom he thought of as a friend. ('I provide the crass and she provides the class,' Elkins said at the time.) Rod and Elkins had met at a party and had enjoyed each other's company. Elkins had often visited Rod at home, roaring up to the house on his powerful motorbike.

Rod made a fateful mistake when he left for Russia to play Napoleon in *Waterloo*. He rang Elkins, asking him to look after Claire while he was away. The result was an intense affair, during which Elkins persuaded her to leave Rod and marry him.

Her new husband characterized Claire as 'a remarkable lady: neurotic, beautiful, superstitious, naïve'. But the marriage turned out to be as fraught as her third, to novelist Philip Roth.

Looking back on her time with Elkins, she wrote, 'He was interested mainly in my bringing home money.' So too was Philip Roth, who demanded that Claire throw out her daughter, Anna, when she was eighteen. Claire later tried to defend her actions on British TV, but the wound was still deep so far as Anna was concerned. 'This is all whitewash,' Anna said. 'You just wanted me out of the way.' She later condemned her mother as 'a narcissistic masochist. Somehow or other, Claire will always come out on top.'

Truth to tell, both Claire and Steiger were at that stage of their careers when both were obsessive about their work. Rod often compared acting to the act of romancing a woman. 'If you are really in love and find her attractive, you can put your heart into it. But if you don't think she's attractive, then you are no more than reciting lines when you tell her she's beautiful. It's the same with a role; you've got to love it to do a good job.'

In his notebooks, he wrote a poem about their problems:

I am of you – as you are of me,
Being so much of one we are different.
Yet there's a difference in us both.
That difference understood, pursued and acquired, with
   respect
Makes us more completely ourselves.

Rod rarely lacked confidence in his dealings with women, or for that matter with anything else. He once broke into full-throated song while romancing a new girlfriend at Chasen's restaurant and continued until the owner threatened to throw him into the street. At a party given by Arthur Loew Jnr, and attended by many of Hollywood's most important personalities, he suddenly announced that he would sing them a song he had written. He did so, making it up as he went along. He was characterized as 'the kind of guy who would play the violin in front of Jascha Heifetz'.

When he invited journalist Aline Mosby to dinner so that she could interview him ('I wore my best earrings. Rod wore a sports shirt and yesterday's whiskers'), he played her some recordings he had made of love poems by e. e. cummings. She seemed disappointed that 'I did not rate a recording of waves breaking on a beach, which I understand he has frequently employed with other females.' But he did read her some of his own poetry:

I exist
Not as a prophet
But as a searcher
One who follows
The instinctive aphorisms of his
Soul.

Perhaps he was listening to the wrong aphorism when he met the woman who was to become his third wife. Sherry Nelson was a former dancer and a racetrack handicapper and they first encountered one another in a bar, Sneaky Pete's. Rod later went back and bought the bar-stools on which they had sat at this meeting. They began living together in 1970. A year later they went through their own form of marriage ceremony. Said Rod, 'We went out on the lawn with some fine wine. We drank it all, smashed the glasses and agreed no matter what we would stay together.'

They finally married in 1973. Sherry signed a pre-nuptial agreement waiving her rights to his money, and Rod sent out printed invitations that made the event sound like a heavy-weight boxing championship. 'This is to announce that due to circumstances beyond our control (having nothing to do with pregnancy but everything to do with panic) a wedding (yes, you read it right) will take place involving Sherry Nelson in the white trunks at 124½ pounds and Rod Steiger in the black trunks (weight unavailable).' It listed the evening's events beginning with 'Getting Drunk', which was followed by 'The Main Event' and 'Sympathy'.

The joke was to misfire six years later, when Sherry filed for divorce and made the marriage sound like a fight. In her divorce petition she claimed that Rod often lost his temper, shouted at her and once gave her a black eye. She claimed that she was entitled to half of his assets for the three years they lived together before the marriage, as well as assets acquired after the marriage. She hired lawyer Marvin Mitchelson to act for her and demanded $2.4 million in settlement, putting Rod's income at around six hundred thousand dollars a year.

After the divorce, Rod next saw Sherry three years later, in a restaurant in the summer of 1981. He told her, 'Well, you cost me a lot of money but you are still one of the best women there ever was.' Their relationship, so far as I could see, seemed to be easier and more relaxed than his marriage with Claire. Once he brought Sherry up to our home in north London and we went out for dinner at a nearby Chinese restaurant. I can scarcely recall what we talked about – we had a lot to drink – but I remember it was so enjoyable that we walked home through a blinding thunderstorm without noticing the rain. We were, as I remember, singing quietly to each other. Or perhaps 'quietly' is the wrong word. But we were fortunate in having kindly neighbours.

PART TWO

BURNING BRIGHT

$-4-$

By 1947 Rod had acquired an Equity card, after playing a bit part in a revival of Bayard Veiller's *The Trial of Mary Dugan*, a hugely successful and commercial courtroom drama. Even so it was not in the theatre that he was to make his reputation as an exciting young actor, but in television.

It was a fortunate time to be an actor in New York, for it was there that were gathered the best new talents: young writers, directors and actors. Many were working in television, which was a new and exciting medium, free of many of the restraints that were affecting Hollywood at the time. Television was live then, and alive with a sense of danger. There were no second takes; you had only one chance to do it right.

'When you did a half-hour show, you did it in five days. And on the fifth day you had a dress rehearsal and were on the air,' Rod remembers. 'The area you worked in was usually very confined: a room, such as a bedroom or a kitchen. You also had the pressure of an opening night, like you were on Broadway and you had to get it right tonight because the critics and the world were watching and if they didn't like you, you were finished. But you had no chance to come back next day and correct things or re-rehearse them – it was the worst pressure you could possibly have: millions of people watching as the little red light went on in the front of the camera.'

Steiger was often nagged by feelings of panic, something that has never left him during his career. He is haunted at such times by a fear of failure, but, paradoxically, that fear is also a source of strength. When I told him that Laurence Olivier was physically sick before a show of any kind, Steiger seemed relieved to be in the same company. Some of his confrères had never admitted to being sick or frightened, perhaps because of macho vanity, so that he felt singular and alone in his fear.

'It gives you energy out of which you can create,' he says. 'Some people are destroyed by it. Something in their character can't quite handle the weight of the fear. They crumple. Those who don't are those who get through. They're the gladiators of the world, the gladiators of art or whatever you want to call them; somehow they control their fear and out of that fear comes an energy that makes them reach heights even they themselves couldn't imagine.

'So there you were in television – small sets, three cameras on you, watching every move you make in front of millions of people for only one time, one chance, and good luck to you, if you didn't make it. *Bonsoir. Bon voyage.* You were gone.'

It was not until 1947 that television began to have an impact on the nation's entertainment. In May that year NBC began its Kraft Television Theater, offering productions of new and old plays; soon it was among the most popular shows on television, not far behind *I Love Lucy*, Jackie Gleason and Ed Sullivan in its viewing figures.

Hollywood, meanwhile, was in a state of near paralysis. Firstly, the HUAC investigation of 'communists' in the industry resulted in the blacklisting of many talents; then the Supreme Court decided in 1948 that the studios should no longer be allowed to own cinemas as well, a ruling that was to bring an end to the dominance of the studio system. Film actors, producers and directors found that their contracts were suddenly terminated as studios cut back on costs.

Steiger describes himself as non-political, yet his social conscience can be outraged. Around that time there was the notorious 'CBS Loyalty Oath' which the TV station's employees had to sign: it was a signing away, thought Steiger, of the right to be free-choice citizens. It was a right-wing incitement to unthinking patriotism.

A meeting was called about it and four hundred and eighty people from all shades of the political spectrum gathered. 'I believe in my country,' orated Steiger. 'I don't have to sign a contract with it.' But nobody backed him up; the silence of the don't-knows greeted his speech. So Steiger stomped offstage, leaving behind the whiff of his first political incendiarism.

His only other political outburst came in a clash with Charlton Heston in the columns of the *Los Angeles Times*. Heston wrote that he was 'appalled' that the American Film Institute had not honoured director Elia Kazan because of his being a friendly witness to the Un-American Activities Committee. Surely, it was time to forget those Washington days of heated controversy?

Steiger's letter said that he, too, was appalled. That actors and writers had been forced to drive cabs and do other work, because they had been blacklisted. Some had even committed suicide. So, this was no time to forget. 'I am appalled, appalled, appalled at what happened then,' he wrote.

Charlton Heston, the voice of Moses and of God, was speech-less. There was no reply.

For New York's actors, directors and writers, the early years of television were a marvellous opportunity to hone their talents. The Philco Television Playhouse, Goodyear Television Playhouse, Kraft Television Theater, Studio One, Robert Montgomery Presents, Revlon Theatre and other, similar, programmes all showcased new plays, so that by the early 1950s there were at least ten new plays a week being shown.

Among the directors working in this new and exciting medium were Delbert Mann, Arthur Penn, Sidney Lumet, John Frankenheimer, Franklin Schaffner and George Roy Hill, who had been a student with Rod at the American Theatre Wing. Besides Rod, the young acting talent included Paul Newman, George C. Scott, Jack Palance, Jack Lemmon, John Cassavetes,

Eli Wallach, Lee Marvin, Rip Torn, Sidney Poitier, Kim Stanley, Joanne Woodward and James Dean. Scripts poured in from the prolific Rod Serling, from Reginald Rose, who had been an advertising copywriter and whose television plays included *Twelve Angry Men*; J. P. Miller, whose *Days of Wine and Roses* became a successful film; Tad Mosel, who was working as an airline clerk; and Paddy Chayefsky, who until then had written sketches for nightclub comedians.

Producer Jerome Hellman said, 'There was an explosive infusion of viable, creative talent at a time when there was a new industry being created, where the need for people was so voracious that virtually anybody with talent, ability and determination could force his way in at the door and be seen. In my judgement it was a moment in time never repeated.'

Director Arthur Penn remembered it as 'this wonderful confluence of superb acting talent, superb writing talent, and really emerging directorial talent.'

Penn remembers:

You went on the air and there was no stopping, come hell or high water. The minute tape came in, that aspect of it went out. And it went from a high-wire act to something on the ground. That high-wire aspect was crucial because it was, Go! Bam! And away we went for an hour or an hour and a half. A lot of guys had heart attacks. A lot of guys had bleeding ulcers. The pressure was enormous.

He felt that New York actors had the edge then, not necessarily because they were better, but 'because they were constantly in training which is a difference', with TV and Broadway theatre.

Live TV functioned, remembered Penn, because 'these were theatre actors, not actors who needed four or five takes. They were able to just get up and go from eight o'clock to nine o'clock without stopping, performing a full play. They had the flexibility, the training, the sense that once they began performing the play, there was no stopping it, and that is what was consistent with live TV. There was no going back. We'd go on at nine and off at ten, and it was a complete living experience.'

A roundabout repertory, in fact.

Actor Richard Kiley liked the fact that live TV had the emotional aspect of theatre coupled with the subtlety that came from close-ups. 'You didn't have to project to the last row in the balcony,' which provided the chance for the actors to display their stage craft while learning their film craft, the relationship between actor and camera.

For Rod, television was what repertory theatre had been for an earlier generation: a place where you could test your talent by playing an immense variety of roles. He was noticed by Fred Coe, who had been manager of new programme development for NBC. Coe was then producer and director of Television Playhouse, sponsored on alternate weeks by Philco and Goodyear. He offered Rod a part with two or three lines to say; a few weeks later, he offered him another, with five or six lines to say. Over the months, his roles got bigger.

He also appeared often on *You Are There*, a CBS series of dramatic recreations of history presented as news, with the network's top newscaster Walter Cronkite acting as its anchor, intoning at the end of each broadcast, 'What sort of day was it? A day like all days, filled with those events that alter and illuminate our lives . . . and you were there'. The roles were varied, ranging from the intense Russian monk Rasputin to the Elizabethan actor Richard Burbage playing Romeo for the first time.

Between 1948 and 1953, Rod acted in more than two hundred and fifty live television plays, a frequent enough presence for leading critic John Crosby to begin a review, 'The other night, I was watching Rod Steiger give one of his usual effortless and persuasive performances . . .'

For Steiger, all this was a movable feast; he was acting wherever he could, picking up crumbs, slurping juicier roles with

71

small theatre groups. At the Equity Library Theater in Harry Brown's *Sound of Hunting*, set in wartime Italy, he played a soldier (the cast also included Martin Balsam). With People's Drama, Inc. he played in *John Brown*, a drama about the abolitionist, written by former shoe-shine boy Theodore Ward and staged in a theatre-in-the-round which was converted from a motzah warehouse on the East Side. On Broadway he played in Ibsen's *An Enemy of the People*, and in a revival of Clifford Odets' *Night Music* he took the role of a middle-aged detective. He was also in a production of the British comedy *Seagulls Over Sorrento*, with Leslie Nielsen.

In between, he would organize readings of new and classic plays at his apartment with friends. Carroll Baker recalled that he would practise a different dialect at each reading, whether or not the part required it. 'In those days, when he read Molière, his accent went from northern Spain to southern Italy, with a bit of Yiddish thrown in, before it settled down in France.'

Says Rod, 'I was lucky. I came along with some sort of talent when television was born and unknown people got a chance to be hired. Big business didn't move into television until about 1955. Before then, nobody was paying too much attention. There were no rules. The sponsors didn't have the grip on the material they have today.'

When his moment came, he was ready for it. 'There are many, many young actors who don't prepare themselves beyond the glossy photo, don't study hard enough or well enough, don't do their homework, and when their good luck arrives, which does not happen that often in the theatrical world, their talent may be ready for it but their technique is not,' says Rod.

He was ready on 24 May 1953, when he played the lead in a play for the Goodyear Television Playhouse which became the most talked-about production in the history of those anthology series. This showed that it was television, more than the theatre or the cinema, that was mirroring its times, providing gritty, realistic drama that, for all its artful contrivance, its audience recognized as real.

The play was *Marty*, a drama about a fat little Bronx butcher who picks up a skinny schoolteacher that his friends regard as 'a dog'. It was the masterpiece of Chayefsky, who strove to reproduce the speech patterns of the ordinary people – 'dialogue as if it had been wire-tapped', as he put it. The great Italian director, Federico Fellini, once told me that his movie about losers and layabouts, *I Vitteloni*, had been inspired by *Marty* and its understanding of the way men gang together in their unknowing need.

One particular exchange in *Marty* was to become almost a catchphrase, when his friend Angie asks Marty, 'Well, what do you feel like doing tonight?' and Marty replies, 'I don't know, Angie. What do you feel like doing?'

The role of Marty had been intended for Kazan's former assistant, Martin Ritt, who later was to become a successful director, notably of *Hud*, starring Paul Newman and Patricia Neal. But in the Cold War atmosphere that then chilled Hollywood and television his career came to a sudden halt when he was blacklisted because of his earlier involvement with the Communist Party. (This was a time an actress could find herself out of work for having sent a congratulatory message to the Moscow Arts Theatre on its fiftieth anniversary; when a top sitcom could lose its sponsors because one of its actors had been named as a communist in the scurrilous pamphlet *Red Channels*; and when the TV networks employed security chiefs to ensure that the political views of writers, actors and directors would not upset the conservative companies who sponsored their shows.) Coe recommended Rod for the role, playing opposite Nancy Marchand as the teacher. Delbert Mann directed.

There was only one problem moment during the broadcast, and Rod's training and his belief in improvisation carried him through it triumphantly. It came when Marty goes to phone the teacher to ask her out. As he put his dime in, Rod allowed

73

himself the luxury of a moment's relaxation to think, It's going well. But as she answered, he realized he'd forgotten his next line. Quickly, he improvised.

'Do you know I called you and I don't know what I called you about,' he said. Nancy Marchand did not panic either. 'Yes?' she said. Rod continued. 'Isn't that funny? Life's funny. I know what I called you about. I'm a silly fool. Like to go to the movies?' He remembers, 'What it looked like on screen was beautiful. But if you improvise in front of forty million people, you've got to have a lot of guts.'

When the show was over, Rod knew that it had been something special. 'You felt it in your bones, you felt it in your blood, in the songs that you were singing in your heart to yourself.'

The next day, he got up and went to get a corn muffin and a cup of coffee at the corner coffee shop. As he walked down West 81st Street, a garbage truck went by and the driver yelled out the window, 'Hey, Marty – how're ya doing?' Two women passed him in the street. 'Marty, how are you?' they asked.

In the coffee shop, as Rod went to the counter, the guy behind it immediately picked up on Angie's dialogue. 'What're you going to have for breakfast today, Marty, what do you feel like doing?' he asked.

'I don't know, Angie,' said Rod. 'What've you got for breakfast today?'

The public impact was enormous. *Time* and *Newsweek* both wrote about it, and producers and writers attempted to reproduce Marty's success with similarly realistic plays featuring ordinary people. As Chayefsky put it, 'There is far more exciting drama in the reasons why a man gets married than in why he murders someone.'

It was a breakthrough year for Rod. The final accolade came in 1953, when he won the Sylvaner Award for the five best performances of the year: as Vishinsky and Rudolph Hess in two episodes of *You Are There*, the gangster Dutch Schultz in a thriller, a radar operator in *My Brother's Keeper*, and, his greatest television triumph, as Marty in Paddy Chayefsky's play. He was so convincing in *My Brother's Keeper*, giving a panic-stricken pilot instructions on making a blind landing, that viewers called to ask whether he was an actor or a real-life radar-man. His only regret was that, later, he lost out on the film of *Marty*, which was to win four Oscars and bring its star, Ernest Borgnine, an Academy award as best actor of 1955.

I once asked Steiger just how disappointed he was at being passed over. 'Hurtful,' was the reply. 'Actors, like writers, are paranoid: I thought it was something I'd done wrong. But, Ernie Borgnine was very good indeed. It was a totally different reading to my own. Oh, yes, he deserved his Oscar. But, then, [chuckle] so did I!'

− 5 −

I n the thirties Hollywood seemed to be governed by old or oldish men, from the brothers Warner to Sam Goldwyn. Today Hollywood executives, recruited from advertising and the agencies, are young men who think that movies only began with their commercial interest in them. Their memories are as short as their nappies. Film schools have a similar amnesia; too often they believe that film studies begin with the trilogy of *Star Wars*. Recently, Steiger went to see a young studio producer, who asked him whether he could do a Southern accent. Rod told him that he'd won an Oscar for playing a role with a Southern accent. *In the Heat of the Night*? Had the producer seen it? No, came the answer.

Even in his fourth decade as an actor, Rod remains out of sympathy with Hollywood. 'Sometimes I think for developed and good actors there's no room in films, because they don't have anything to challenge them after a while, especially if they get over forty, fifty years old,' he said.

New Yorker critic, Pauline Kael, made the same point in her review of his performance in *No Way to Treat a Lady*, highlighting a problem that has plagued him for much of his career: 'Rod Steiger's presence is so strong that he often seems to take over a picture even when he isn't the lead. This is true of George C. Scott too, and actors this powerful just don't fit into ordinary roles. The answer, of course, is that they need extraordinary ones − great roles. Hollywood's answer is to offer them star turns.'

As a young actor of importance, making his way in theatre and television, Steiger was anxious to break into films. It was an ambition shared by most of his generation of actors. He would hang out at Cromwell's Pharmacy in the lobby of the NBC building at Rockefeller Plaza, a drugstore where many actors, writers and directors gathered to drink coffee, phone their agents, gossip and discuss possible assignments. Among them was a skinny young man, six years his junior, who had an intense admiration for Marlon Brando. Rod and the boy, James Dean, acted together in *The Evil Within*, a science-fiction play in the series *Tales of Tomorrow*, about a scientist, played by Rod, whose wife drinks a serum by mistake and turns into a killer. Dean played his assistant.

Another regular was an ambitious young writer, Stewart Stern. A New Yorker who was three years older than Rod, he had begun as an actor before the war, then served in the infantry and, when he returned to civilian life, had begun writing scripts for Television Playhouse. He was determined to work in films, where he had an entrée of sorts – his cousin was Arthur Loew Jnr, who was then the youngest producer at MGM, a studio founded by his grandfather Marcus Loew. Stern was hired by director Fred Zinnemann to write a script for his film *Teresa*, loosely based on Alfred Hayes's novel *The Girl on the Via Flaminia*, which was the story of an Italian girl who goes to New York with her GI husband and is soon at war with his domineering mother.

Stern had an eye for acting talent. He suggested that seventeen-year-old Pier Angeli would be ideal to play the girl and recommended Rod for a small role as an army psychiatrist. This was an indicator of the two-way traffic in experience that an actor's life is all about: his own knowledge of the psychiatrist's couch was invaluable to him when he came to play the fictional character. Rod has reason to remember Zinnemann's kindness and consideration to him on his film debut. He found the experience nerve-racking. 'I didn't know what I was doing, and the absence of knowledge is the foundation of fear,' he says. 'I had trouble getting through my part.'

When the time came for a break on his first day, Zinnemann invited Rod to accompany him to lunch. Rod, flattered, agreed, and was even more flattered when Zinnemann asked Rod how he thought he was doing as a director.

> I was a cocky young kid, and I proceeded to tell him that he was a very fine director and knew what he wanted, but perhaps he didn't know enough about acting and acting technique to get what he wanted. And I carried on with my dissertation about how he should get more familiar with the techniques and mechanics of acting and I felt pretty good.
>
> It was only years later that I realized he was being a good director, who should be like a father to his family. He took me to lunch and was relaxing me for the day's work. I'll never forget his warmth and generosity and how he took care of me.

The director considered Rod to be the quintessential Method actor. He was, Zinnemann wrote in his autobiography, 'very popular, extremely articulate and full of remarkable theories'. But when Rod came to play his scene, he forgot his lines. The crew, Zinnemann remembered, found the moment very funny; they were 'behind schedule and under pressure and needed a good laugh'.

Steiger was less amused. He decided that he was not yet ready for films and he would not act in one again until he felt he could do justice to himself and the role.

His love of Zinnemann, though, continued throughout life. Every time he visited London, where Zinnemann had retired with a serious illness, he visited him, telling me how Zinnemann was and how he was terrified that his classic showdown movie, *High Noon*, might be remade – in colour. 'They can't do that, can they?' he asked Steiger. Steiger said he hoped they couldn't.

But, of course, the crassness of commerce in Hollywood can be overwhelming; there are always good reasons for doing the wrong things.

Early on, Steiger determined that he would be his own man, choosing his roles carefully, which also meant becoming well enough known to be offered the roles in the first place. As a result he was determined not to sign any long-term contract with a studio or production company which would limit his freedom of choice. He thought his moment had arrived following his success as Marty in Paddy Chayefsky's television play. Among the admiring television audience was Harold Hecht, a one-time dancer and actor who had become an agent; his great achievement had been guiding the career of Burt Lancaster from minor New York actor to major Hollywood star. He and Lancaster had set up their own production company, Hecht–Lancaster, the year before and they were looking for material.

Hecht was impressed by *Marty* and decided that he wanted to produce a film version. Chayefsky agreed to add scenes to the original television script, which had run for only fifty minutes or so, in order to bring it up to the ninety minutes required for a feature. (The final cut of the film ran for ninety-one minutes, which just proves Chayefsky's professionalism.)

Hecht signed Delbert Mann to direct again. (Mann's second feature was also to be a play he had first done on television, Paddy Chayefsky's *Bachelor Party*.) Both Mann and Chayefsky wanted Rod to play Marty once more, but Lancaster was worried that audiences wouldn't pay to see a feature film which seemed to be no more than a repeat of the television play.

Steiger began to grow anxious and phoned Chayefsky. 'Paddy, we stick together we can do this, y'know?' he said. Chayefsky's reply startled him: 'I can only fight so much for you, Rod. I need the credit,' he said. Rod, upset, said, 'I hope you get the credit,' and hung up the phone.

'I was told that some people were afraid to use me because I improvise a lot and they didn't know what I was going to do, or what I would say. But it worked well for them when I did it,' he says.

Steiger was invited to meet Lancaster and Hecht. They offered him the role on condition that he signed a seven-year contract with them. Rod asked who would choose his roles. When they said that they would, Rod refused to sign. He told them that he had the right to make his own mistakes, that you cannot take the right of choice away from a person.

Harold Hecht and Burt Lancaster were a curious pair; both of them had an unerring, if wary, eye for the sure thing, such as Clifford Odets' *The Sweet Smell of Success*. The Scottish director, Alexander Mackendrick, who directed that film for them, once told me that he went to a meeting in their skyscraper office. Hecht and Lancaster disagreed about something, so, hardly pausing in conversation, the muscle-bound Lancaster picked the smaller Hecht up and held him out of the window until Hecht agreed to what was under discussion. Mackendrick goggled. 'We solve most of our arguments like that,' confided Lancaster.

It's possible the pair made the offer of a contract in the knowledge that Rod would reject it. Lancaster already had Ernest Borgnine, an experienced film actor, in mind for the role; the two had worked together on *From Here to Eternity*. *Marty* not only brought Borgnine an Academy award, but also brought a change in the parts offered him. Until that time, he had tended to be cast as a 'heavy': a sadistic sergeant in *From Here to Eternity* and the town bully in *Bad Day at Black Rock*. After *Marty*, he appeared in mainly good-hearted and cheerful roles. It was Rod who was to become typecast as a villain.

A few days after the TV showing of *Marty*, Rod bumped into Kazan. 'What the hell did you do on Sunday with that *Marty*?' he asked. 'Everybody's talking about it. Why don't you go up and see Budd Schulberg?' and he gave him an address.

Schulberg was busy working with Kazan on a new film which he had scripted from his novel. Rod was invited to read for the part of a mob lawyer, who needed to look like he could be the brother of Marlon Brando, already cast in the leading role. Originally, Lawrence Tierney had been approached to play the part, but he wanted more money than Kazan was prepared to pay. Rod was excited by the opportunity. He'd seen Brando in *A Streetcar Named Desire* and had been impressed.

'I felt lucky on one hand that I had the opportunity and I was scared to death on the other,' Rod recalls, when Schulberg told him the role was his. 'Mr Kazan was the hottest director in town and Mr Brando the hottest actor in the United States and maybe the world. I wasn't afraid of doing my scenes, but I was nervous about doing them well.'

As it turned out, he was to do them brilliantly. The film was *On the Waterfront*, which was not only to become a classic of American cinema, but included a scene – a confrontation between Rod and Brando – that was destined to be the most discussed moment in any film ever made, endlessly dissected and analysed over the years by critics and students alike. Some of the discussion has suggested that there had been bad feeling between Rod and Brando during the film's making. But when Maria Schneider, Brando's co-star in *Last Tango in Paris*, was interviewed in the *New York Times* in 1973, candidly discussing Brando's performance in that film, Rod wrote a letter to the paper, protesting about her 'unnecessary revelations concerning Marlon Brando's private life, choice, vanities, physique or what have you'.

On the Waterfront, in 1954, won a whole raft of Academy awards for everyone except Steiger. Most notable in acting terms was Brando, whose role as Terry Malloy revealed a character whose hard-boiled façade as an ex-boxer hid a heart (a love of homing pigeons) and a conscience (Eva Marie Saint urges him to rise above the crooked union of longshoremen). It is, in fact – and this is not to deny its brilliance – an apologia for being witnesses to the Un-American Activities Committee. Both Kazan and Schulberg had moved over the edge of betrayal of comrades

– something which Steiger, now, despises intensely – and there is, in fact, a priest (Karl Malden) who urges informing upon his congregation as a Christian act. Judas as Jesus, in fact.

But there is still no denying the power of what might have been a Terrytoon of caricature for Brando (from William Holden to Robert Montgomery, Hollywood has usually treated boxers as either muscle-bound idealists or brain-mashed pugs). Kazan and Schulberg gave Brando a remarkable march for greatness. He took it.

Brando had been established as one of the great men of Hollywood, despite the disparity between his private life-style and public mannerisms. His attitude made him the grit in the machine. But his success made him the machine.

Although Oscar-less, Rod Steiger's performance was no less notable. His role, brief as it was, had enormous impact for the movie and his own future. He played the part of Charlie, the corrupt, soft-living lawyer-brother to Terry; the elder sibling who sorted the deals made by the union boss, played by Lee J. Cobb. Charlie laundered the public aspect of the union and had persuaded brother Terry to take a dive in a championship fight because the bets were running the other way. As Terry says bitterly in the film, 'I could have been a contender.'

A notable villain? Steiger gave it more than that, in projecting a man compromised not just by a way of life but by his own unknowing defects. A Shakespearean anti-hero almost, with a night-club pallor to indicate where the loot has been spent.

When, in the back of that cab, he draws a gun and Terry waves it away, it is a decisive act which has settled his fate.

On the Waterfront was very important to Steiger's career. As a film it can be seen now to have flaws and its energy shoots off in too many directions at once. But, says Steiger, 'We knew we were on to a hot one. We were generous to each other as actors and technicians. We knew it was going to be a fine movie. Except of course for Mr Brando; generosity was not the name of his game.'

As critic Richard Schickel has pointed out, no one attempted to build on the success of *On the Waterfront*, even though the performances assured the ascendancy of a particular acting style. Brando and Steiger would 'become characters in search of auteurs who did not exist'. They needed the great roles. And by the time there was a new generation of directors – Coppola and Scorsese among them – willing to take up where Kazan had left off, there was also a new generation of actors, including Robert De Niro and Al Pacino, to play the roles.

Steiger, like Dean, was a product of the Actors' Studio. Like others turned out by this powerhouse of a new style of acting, although they would listen respectfully to their teachers, once they were working, whether it was in theatre, television or film, they tended to question directors and gained a reputation for awkwardness. Elia Kazan, one of the Studio's founders, called them 'a curiously ambitious and restlessly searching kind of actor'. They were taught to be proud, which did not always make them easy to work with. They tended to ignore the instructions of directors who they regarded as incompetent. Brando tested each new director by doing a scene in two different ways – once with feeling, once without – and seeing whether the director could tell the difference. 'Never give a stupid, egotistical, insensitive or inept director an even break,' he remarked. Rod, too, was to develop a similar approach which, in the long term, probably hampered his career.

As director Robert Aldrich put it, discovering that Rod's habit of altering what he said often confused other actors: 'Usually I lie awake nights trying to think of ways to improve an actor's performance. With Steiger, the problem is to try and contain him.'

The flamboyant director Samuel Fuller formed the same opinion when he made *Run of the Arrow* in 1957, starring Rod as a Confederate soldier who joins the Sioux rather than submit to the North. Rod insisted on playing the role as an Irishman.

Fuller, who had worked as a tabloid crime reporter and served in the infantry during the war, taking part in the Normandy invasion, was a tough and exuberant director, who liked to surprise his actors during filming. Occasionally, he would arrive on set with a loaded revolver and shoot it in the air.

He thought that Steiger was good, providing he was kept under control. Rod preferred to work with directors who allowed him more freedom and has never cared for the film, though its reputation has grown over the years.

'I read up about the South and found that it was settled by the Scots and the English and the Irish. So I go ahead and do the first Irish Cowboy. And you try saying, "They went thataway" with an Irish accent in front of an audience,' Rod told me.

Steiger has tried his hand at screenwriting, finishing several scripts that he hoped he might be able to direct. The problem has always been finding finance outside Hollywood. 'Nothing I have written could be done in Hollywood,' he told an audience at a film seminar. 'Nor would I want to direct a film there. The Hollywood director is the centre of such awful pressure that I think I might buckle, break down, blow my brains out.'

The pressure of his own life, though, was enough to bring him to the brink of that implosion. For him, life was always a loaded gun of the kind Sam Fuller loved.

− 6 −

Rod's screen role in *On the Waterfront* was one that was to haunt him for the rest of his career, and helped to typecast him in tough, villainous roles. When I wrote a profile of Steiger for the *Guardian* newspaper, he rang to complain: 'But you always see me as a heavy!' *On the Waterfront* had characterized him in that way. And it's worth commenting on it again, as it was so seminal to his future career.

Its director, Elia Kazan, was strong enough not to be intimidated either by its star, Marlon Brando, or by Rod, unlike some directors in his future, who were often to feel that he was trying to take over the film from them. 'I'm not trying to take over,' Rod insists. 'I'm trying to take the medium of acting to as far as I can go, and that's why sometimes I go over the edge.'

As Charlie, a mob lawyer, brother to Brando's prizefighter turned longshoreman, he recognized similarities between Charlie and his former role, Marty, in that both involved a struggle between good and bad impulses within a man. Both also have in common, he wrote, 'a basic sound American education in a democratic school system that affords an opportunity for the individual to make a choice between "good" and "evil".' It was also the first time that the improvisatory technique learned at the Actors' Studio came into full cinematic play – and worked.

During the first days on the set, he felt nervous. But there came a moment when he ad-libbed and released the tension he was feeling. It happened when he and Brando were in a scene together. Brando was looking at a girlie magazine and turning the pages so fast Rod could not see them. So he asked, 'Would you go back again, I'd like to see that?' And Brando turned back the pages, a spontaneous moment that made it into the final cut.

As I have said, it was the final confrontation between the two, in the back of a taxi-cab, that has become a classic scene in American cinema. At this point, Rod is prepared to kill his brother unless he stops opposing the methods of the mob-controlled union. As they take their final ride together, Terry reproaches Charlie for his behaviour.

James Naremore in his *Acting in the Cinema* has hailed this as 'a touchstone of American film acting, and one of the best-remembered moments in either player's career.' It was instantly recognized as a classic, so much so that Mike Nichols and Elaine May, then a comedy duo, performed the taxi-cab conversation in the style of Louisa M. Alcott as the climax to an improvised routine.

The scene was a convincing demonstration of the power of a new style of acting. But there is some truth in Naremore's contention that this bravura display showed that 'Method acting, a system of training that aims to transcend mere play acting, depends, at bottom, on a star system.' As he points out, 'an apparent search for "truth" and "authenticity" had turned into a showcase for technique.'

The setting for that taxi sequence was the result of an accident or, rather, the renowned parsimony of Sam Spiegel, an impulsive and adventurous producer, but one who preferred to spend his money on himself. 'He looked as if he'd just got off his camel somewhere, he could sell you anything,' says Rod. 'And he produced some wonderful things, a man of taste above all. Wily, strong, prepossessed with ambition, a lover of women, but a man of taste, always.'

He was, though, in many ways, a typical producer. One freezing morning, at around three a.m., when Eva Marie Saint, Lee J. Cobb, Karl Malden, Elia Kazan and Rod were sitting round in a small hotel in Hoboken during a break in the filming, Spiegel swept in, dressed as ever, in a vicuna coat.

He took Kazan into the adjoining room, but the actors overheard the heated exchange quite clearly. What they heard was Spiegel saying, 'I don't care about the actors. Beat them. Hit them. Kill them. Starve them, but get the goddamn picture done.'

With that, he came back into the room, lighting a cigar as he passed and climbed into his limousine waiting outside. 'Good evening, ladies and gentlemen,' he said as he left, as if nothing untoward had happened. The actors felt as if someone had poured iced water over them.

Spiegel himself, though, could be intimidated. I remember talking to him about the Marlon Brando movie, *The Chase*, which he produced. It was directed by Arthur Penn and written by the tough old lady of American literature, Lillian Hellman. She had wanted one scene done her way and she got it. Said Spiegel: 'She had more balls than Brando, Penn and me put together. I was shit-scared of her.'

Originally Kazan had wanted to film the confrontation scene in a real taxi in real traffic, but Spiegel had refused because of the cost. He promised instead the shell of an old taxi, together with back projection equipment showing a street scene through the cab's windows to give the illusion of movement.

But all Kazan had, when he came to film the scene, was the back part of a cab and a steering wheel for Nehemiah Persoff, who was playing the taxi driver. There was no rear projection equipment and the room was so narrow that Rod could put his arms out the windows of the cab and touch the walls on either side. 'There was nothing to represent a street, or traffic, or buildings,' he recalls.

Kazan was screaming at Spiegel, who was trying to calm him. Then a technician mentioned that the taxi he had used that morning had had a venetian blind over the back window. Kazan sent out for one immediately. But that still left him with a problem: he could not shoot the scene so that the side-windows were visible because it would have shown the bare walls beyond. As a result he had to come in close on Brando and Rod, which added to the intensity of the scene.

It is often said that the scene was improvised – indeed, Brando claims as much in his autobiography – but that is inaccurate, as an examination of the shooting script will reveal. At the beginning, during rehearsals, Brando began to improvise and Rod followed suit – until Kazan yelled, 'Stop the shit, Buddy', which was what Brando's friends called him. After that, they both stuck to the words Budd Schulberg had written.

The scene took eleven hours to film. When it came to do Brando's close-ups, Rod stood off-camera and said his lines. 'A lot of acting is re-acting so it's always good to have the actor playing opposite you off-stage because you have a chance to react to something,' Rod said.

But when it was time for Rod to do his close-ups, Brando went home. According to Kazan, he had an appointment with his psychiatrist, though at the time he told Rod that Brando was tired. Brando did not explain himself to Rod. He just disappeared. It was to take Rod many years to forgive him.

'I couldn't believe that Elia Kazan, one of the best directors around, would let Marlon go home. I wouldn't believe that Marlon *wanted* to go home,' says Rod. 'All I know is I had to do my close-up without him and I never quite got over that, and even childishly to this day I feel angry.'

He certainly felt angry at the time, accusing Kazan of indulging Brando. Kazan tried to make amends by reading Brando's lines to Rod. Rod's feelings weren't assuaged when, later, in *The Duke in his Domain*, a profile for the *New Yorker*, Truman Capote asked Brando about the scene. Brando replied, 'That scene. Let me see. There were seven takes because Rod Steiger couldn't stop crying. He's one of those actors who loves to cry. We kept doing it over and over.' It was, thought Rod, who stayed dry-eyed throughout the film, an unfair and unkind remark.

Brando was helpful in one scene, where Rod has been killed by his gangland associates and hung on a hook in an alleyway. Brando has to lift the body off the hook. The filming was done on location in New Jersey on a freezing night. It was so cold that the camera froze, despite heat lamps to keep it warm, and filming had to stop to thaw it out. Rod's problem was that Brando was taking his time in removing him from the hook, longer than it was possible for him to hold his breath – and his breath could be seen, especially under the bright lights that were being used to film the scene.

'I thought Marlon would never get me off the hook as he did his reacting and carrying on,' said Rod. Once he was off the hook and slung over Brando's shoulder, Rod was able to take a breath because his mouth was buried in Brando's coat. It was Brando who suggested he took a lot of quick breaths, hyperventilating so that he could fill his body with oxygen and hold his breath for a longer period. It worked. 'I still felt as though my lungs were going to burst,' he remembers.

Rod's estimation of Brando as an actor remains high. 'I have great respect for him,' he says. He remembers sitting through three showings of one of his performances, trying to discover what it was that gave him such a charismatic presence.

I realized there was part of him always churning with something, some problem he was dealing with. I got the impression of a man who was trying to solve the pain of something – perhaps he was gifted with or burdened with – that he didn't really want, or he didn't want it, so long as he didn't understand it. It kept him, whether he liked it or not, continually alert, seeking for a solution and continually alive, and connected with all of us who have things inside of us going on all the time, and we became fascinated, unconsciously, and watched his turmoil. And that's the word. Turmoil. It was a continuing deep and personal problem.

Schulberg's script, and his novel, had ended with Brando's character dead, floating down the river. But the Hays Office objected, on the grounds that it would give the impression of crime being triumphant. So an ending in which Brando is beaten but survives was substituted.

Later, Rod was amused to read a review that treated the film as an allegory of Christ, insisting that Brando's fight at the end had been his march to Calvary, mimicking the Stations of the Cross. In reality, it was Kazan improvising a new ending. 'March to Calvary? We were just trying to get out of a hole,' said Rod.

Rod's performance was much admired, for what Richard Schickel called 'the unctuously patronizing manner, not quite covering the clammy fear in which he has lived all his life'. More importantly for his reputation in Hollywood, he had been associated with a box-office success. *On the Waterfront* had cost $902,000 and grossed $9,500,000. And he was one of three from the cast, along with Lee J. Cobb and Karl Malden, to be nominated for an Oscar as best supporting actor (although the award went to Edmond O'Brien in *The Barefoot Contessa*). The film took eight Oscars, including best picture, best supporting actress for Eva Marie Saint, and a best actor award for Brando.

There was finally a kind of resolution to the rancour that Steiger felt for Marlon Brando over the years since that act of treachery in *On the Waterfront*.

In Montreal, Canada, in 1997, Steiger was to receive a lifetime achievement award – 'they're so kind, but they throw these things around like confetti when you're my age' – and he heard that Brando was also in town. Although invited to the ceremony he did not attend. Par for the course.

But that night Steiger went to a plush Chinese restaurant – Chinese and Italian food are his delights – and there, in a corner seat, plumped up like the vast cushion he has become through gorging on his life and his career, was Brando. He was surrounded by disciples. He saw Steiger; he waved; he tried to get up, but his great weight made it difficult.

Steiger walked over to him and they shook hands and they embraced and they rubbed balding heads together in affection. They were both in tears. They mumbled words which, now, Steiger professes to have forgotten.

Then they let each other go. Steiger, though, had the last word.

'It's dreadful. Terrible. Awful.'

'What is?' asked Marlon Brando.

'Well,' said Steiger. 'We'll never again be able to say nasty, unkind things about each other after a reconciliation like this!'

So, they parted – each to their chow mein and sweet and sour remembrances of times past.

The success of Steiger's next film, although it gave him the opportunity to display his singing voice and even dance, was to trap him in 'heavy' roles for some considerable time. Physically, he was ideally suited to play villains; he was a burly, threatening, overpowering presence. But he longed to play more romantic and gentler roles.

He was asked by Fred Zinnemann to screen test for the role of Jud Fry in *Oklahoma!*, a film of Rodgers and Hammerstein's folksy musical that had a revolutionary effect on the Broadway musical theatre from its opening in March 1943. Jud – 'a bullet-coloured, growly man', as the musical's hero Curly calls him – is the villain of the piece. Another Actors' Studio regular, Eli Wallach, was also in the running for the role.

At that stage, Zinnemann was hoping to use actors rather than singers in the leading roles. Montgomery Clift as Curly, and Eva Marie Saint as Laurey were among the names mentioned. He asked Rod to do a test with another actor he was considering for the role of Curly.

But when Paul Newman was late, he substituted James Dean, who impressed Zinnemann, though the role eventually went to a more conventional performer, but a better singer, Gordon MacRae. Part of the deal was that Rodgers and Hammerstein had final approval of the cast.

'There was no opposition to my choice of Rod Steiger as the sinister hired man Jud,' Zinnemann has said.

I was seduced by his brilliant talent into exploring the character's underlying motives rather than playing him as the straight, despicable musical villain whom everyone loves to hate. As a result he emerged as a disturbed, isolated person shunned by everyone, and this seduced the audience into a kind of reluctant pity; perhaps unconsciously they felt sorry for Jud, and when he died, the jubilation of the community was not echoed by the relief in the audience.

Since there were too many oil wells spoiling the wide, open country of Oklahoma itself, the film was shot on location, mainly in Nogales, Arizona.

Rod did not care for the location. On one of his first days there, he went for a dip in the hotel swimming pool. As he put his hand on the side to get out, he heard a voice say with great authority, 'Don't move!'

He froze, hanging on to the side of the pool in the deep end, not knowing what the danger was. He heard footsteps running, a door bang, footsteps coming back. Then there was a gunshot that deafened him. 'I looked over where my right hand was, and about a foot away from it was a small snake, about twelve inches long, striped like a barber pole.' It was a coral snake, whose bite is inevitably fatal.

After that, Rod caused much amusement to Oscar Hammerstein and his wife by always wearing his cowboy boots with his bathing briefs when he walked by the side of the pool. 'I looked like a cross between King Kong and Porky Pig running around in those boots.'

Steiger's interpretation of Jud was that he was really in love with Laurey. Whether he knew it or not, he was obsessed by her, and the obsession kills him.

'Sometimes in acting it's very good to ask yourself, if there was another scene in this picture, if this story went on, what would have happened to the characters around you? And it's a way of playing with your imagination, a way of revitalizing it, so you might get some more insight or come up with an exciting conception about a part,' he says.

'When you're really working hard, you do it before and after each scene. You ask yourself, what happened before? You must know what's happening before, always, but you can imagine, what if this happened before? Or what if this happened after? It can help activate your imagination for the scene that you're working on.

'I figured that if Jud hadn't fallen on his knife when he did, and they'd picked him up and controlled him, it would have been too late for him. His mind would have snapped; he would have been a raving idiot. And he would have been confined to an institution. That was my concept.'

But he also thought that Jud's problems, unlike those of the Charlie and Marty characters, stemmed from his lack of education. 'Deep down in our hearts the audience feels that if Jud had had equal opportunities of democratic education, as most of us have had, a happier solution would have been accomplished, as it was in the case of Marty,' he wrote in a newspaper article on the film.

Rod was attracted to Shirley Jones who was playing the heroine, Laurey. 'She was so healthy, it was frightening for Godsakes, and full of vitality. She had a lovely voice and was intelligent.'

Then Fred Zinnemann took him aside and asked him to keep an eye on her. 'Protect her, she's young, she's never done a film before and just be like a brother to her,' he asked. So that is what he did, and any chance of romance was over before it could begin. When not being brotherly, he spent his time with Eddie Albert, who had a great skill in mixing cocktails.

Rod's most nerve-racking moment was while recording his duet with the accomplished Gordon MacRae, on Stage 25 at the

MGM studios, a huge hangar of a place with, at the far end of it, a microphone and a pair of headphones.

He looked around in confusion. Had he come to the right place? There was no orchestra in sight. And where was Gordon MacRae? Then a voice came over the sound system: 'Hello, Rod, we're glad you're here, put the earphones on, we'll begin.'

'Where's Gordon?' he asked. 'Where's the orchestra?'

'They've already recorded,' came the reply.

'I don't know what kept me from fainting,' he recalls.

I said a very weak 'Oh – oh, aha, that's nice,' and I walk over, and I put on the earphones, and all of a sudden I hear 'BOM-BOM-BA-BOM', and it's like the London Symphony Orchestra playing 'POOR-JUD-IS-DEAD'.

I must have lost a hundred and thirty-five pounds as I stood in front of that microphone. I guess I did it in under an hour and I was apologizing to people and they said, 'Get out of here, we have opera singers come here have to do one note at a time' and stuff like that.

Agnes de Mille had been hired to restage her dance sequences, notably her ballet of Laurey's dream of Jud and Curly that had been a sensational success in the stage version. 'She is one of the most dedicated, sensitive, compassionate, artistic people I have ever met,' says Rod. 'I don't know what the word "artistic" means, but if it means caring for humanity, and wanting to alleviate humanity's pain by giving it a gift of some beauty, this woman is one of the great ones at exchanging gifts with the world. She's just marvellous.'

The stars were replaced in the dream ballet by professional dancers. Shirley Jones was danced by Bambi Linn, who had been in the Broadway production, and Gordon MacRae by James Mitchell. But Rod noticed that there was no dancer to represent Jud. The problem was that they could not find a dancer who resembled him in size.

Then one day he got a call from Agnes de Mille to say she had found someone to dance the role. He hurried down to see her, and asked, 'Where's this guy who looks like me? Who is it?'

And she said, 'You!'

'Don't be silly,' he told her. 'I can't dance.'

'Can you count to four?' she asked.

'Don't be ridiculous, of course I can count to four: one, two, three, four,' Rod said.

'Then you can dance,' she said, counting 'one, two, three, four,' as she did some simple movements.

'So I did the ballet,' Steiger says.

When you see the picture obviously it's me. I didn't dream I could do that. The only thing that saved me in the ballet was that the man had to be lumbering and awkward, and I was gifted to be lumbering and awkward. I always, to this day, joke with other actors. I say, listen, a lot of other actors can say they acted a part, and they sang a part, and they danced a part. But how many actors can say they acted a part, they sang a part, and they did the ballet of the part?

His most testing moment came when he had to lift Bambi Linn over his head. He was worried that he might drop her and she would break a leg and he would have ruined her career. It wasn't merely that he had to lift her once or twice, but more than twenty times as takes were filmed from different angles. Thank God I delivered ice when I was a boy and had some little muscles left in my rear end, he thought to himself:

If actors worked as hard as dancers at their craft we would have acting beyond the sublime. Actors are lazy slobs, myself included. They do not exercise, they don't even vocalize, they don't do anything, they don't do enough of their homework in my opinion – I believe that eighty per cent of the acting today would be much better if actors did more of their home-work and had more discipline. We stagger in some mornings, half-asleep, groping for coffee, groping for the first cigarette, hoarse-voiced.

The dancer can't do that. If the body is not warmed up, they're gonna sprain a muscle or break a leg or something. So they have no choice but to be disciplined. And I wish it was that way for actors, myself included, I think my work and other people's might be a helluva lot better.

Rod's performance, lowering and darkly menacing, brought a reality to the part that is not often seen within the somewhat artificial world of the musical. Said Zinnemann, 'Rod transformed Jud into a modern neurotic and made people feel sorry for him.'

But humiliation was to follow soon after this success, since Rod was asked by Rodgers and Hammerstein to repeat his performance, together with Shirley Jones as Laurey, in a special theatrical presentation of the musical in Italy. 'Hammerstein was a cross between Abraham Lincoln and Will Rogers – the dignified and the droll – Rodgers was a cool, methodical, distant person,' says Rod.

Steiger was aware that he might have problems, with his penchant for changing key without realizing it. 'Since I had sung the song in the picture and got away with it I guess they figured I could, and I figured I'd take a chance, too.'

He found the rehearsals difficult, was perspiring freely and losing weight with worry. The moment came when the cast did its first run through, with both Rodgers and Hammerstein sitting in the auditorium, listening. When they finished, Rod heard Rodgers' voice coming to him out of the darkness, 'You know, Rod, if there's cancer, you've got to cut it out.' Rod was confused. 'I beg your pardon?' he said. 'We're going to have to let you go,' was Rodgers' response.

'Couldn't you have put it in a nicer way?' asked Rod. 'Couldn't

96

Bearded in his den – Steiger and Akim Tamiroff. Tamiroff was a great character actor whose character saved many a movie.

Steiger as fashion plate. Baron, Britain's best-known photographer of the time, softened that hard-man image in 1957.

(*Opposite*) Steiger in deep thought – or predatory mood – in *13, West Street* (1962), an early version of the *Death Wish* idea. It co-starred Alan Ladd in what was to be his penultimate movie.

What the well-dressed gangster is wearing: fedora, smart collar and tie, carnation and scar. One of Steiger's best: a low-key portrayal of Al Capone, back in 1959.

Steiger emoting to some effect as the viciously crooked boxing manager in *The Harder They Fall* (1956). Humphrey Bogart (his last film) and Mike Lane are in more contemplative mood.

Brotherly love was never so evident as in *On the Waterfront*, when Steiger draws a gun on younger brother Marlon Brando – in an attempt to save his life.

(*Opposite*) A trio of temperaments. Three of the most important screen actors of the day (*from left to right*), Lee J. Cobb, Marlon Brando and Steiger in *On the Waterfront* (1954).

The Illustrated Man (1969). 'The make-up took hours,'
Steiger recalls. 'It was not a good feeling.'

(*Opposite*) Murder most camp. Steiger as the mother-loving woman-killer in
No Way to Treat a Lady (1968). One of his greatest 'all-risks' performances.

(*Overleaf*) Julie Christie with Steiger in David Lean's plush and romantic view
of Boris Pasternak's *Doctor Zhivago* (1965).

you have called me down privately and told me?' He had never felt so humiliated. He began to weep, not with sorrow, but in fury. He walked around the auditorium four times to keep himself from punching Rodgers for his insensitivity. Finally, he rushed to a side exit.

'I just smashed through a door,' he says. 'I don't know to this day whether it was supposed to open or not but it opened for me. And I never went back. That was the first and last time in my life that I was fired.'

But the word was good on his acting in the film. *Variety* pronounced it a 'socko performance', adding that he brought to the part of Jud 'all the dark menace it requires'. David Selznick was impressed enough to try to sign Rod to a long-term contract and as a possible lead for *A Farewell to Arms*. Rod recalls: 'But I told him that I must have the right to choose my own mistakes. His face fell – he couldn't believe anyone could refuse him. Neither could my agents!' Gossip columnist Sheila Graham and others tipped Rod for an Oscar nomination.

Rod followed *Oklahoma!* with a role as a sneering baddie in *Jubal*, which was based vaguely on *Othello*. Shakespeare's tragedy of jealousy and revenge had been transferred to a Western setting by novelist Paul Wellman. Rod had the Iago-like part of Pinky, a foreman who encourages a rancher to believe that his wife is attracted to a wandering cowboy. Pinky's motivation isn't simply a matter of abstract hatred, as was Iago's, but because he himself is the wife's former lover.

Steiger did not enjoy his role, clashing from the start with director and screenwriter Delmer Daves, who preferred the laconic, tightly controlled style of the film's star, Glenn Ford. (He and Ford went on to make two more Westerns together in the next two years.) Daves accused Rod of overacting, but the producer William Fadiman liked what he saw in the rushes and told Daves to let Rod play the role his way.

The cast also included Ernest Borgnine as the rancher and

Canadian actress Valerie French as the wife, who, unlike Shake-speare's Desdemona, amply justifies her husband's jealousy. Rod's performance, in which he rapes the wife and almost hangs her lover, dominated the film, and received an accolade from Valerie French's husband, the English screenwriter and play-wright Michael Pertwee, who called him 'the best villain we've had in years'.

That view was echoed by *Variety*'s critic: 'Steiger, who has changed his accent but not his act, spews an evil venom over the footage as the drawling cowhand who wants the ranch and the rancher's wife. There hasn't been as hateful a screen heavy around in a long time.'

Rod took the role for two reasons – the money, which was twice as much as he had ever earned before – and the power it would give him to choose his future roles. 'It automatically put me in a different income bracket. You know what happens then? Suddenly it's "Mr Steiger". Now I don't care whether people call me Mister or not, but I do care about having a say in what I'm doing. And when they call you Mister, you get that say.'

The second film Rod made in 1955 was *The Court-Martial of Billy Mitchell*, directed by Otto Preminger in a bad-tempered production. Rod again took the acting honours as a clever prose-cuting attorney, despite a cast that included such veteran stars and scene-stealers as Gary Cooper, Charles Bickford and Ralph Bellamy. The film, re-titled *One Man Mutiny* in Britain, was an attack on military bureaucracy, based on the true story of Mit-chell who predicted the Japanese attack on Pearl Harbor sixteen years before it happened.

Variety's critic warmed to him: 'Steiger sneers, jeers and figu-ratively knees the defendant with a fine you'll-love-to-hate-me zestiness,' he reported. Ruth Waterbury, critic for the *Los Angeles Examiner*, thought his acting was 'just fantastic'.

He followed it with another searing performance, playing a man with no redeeming qualities whatsoever: Stanley Hoff, the megalomaniacal boss of a film studio in Robert Aldrich's film of *The Big Knife*, from Clifford Odets' play.

Some audiences regarded the film as a lurid fantasy, but it was close to the truth of Hollywood. Rod's character was based on the tough and abrasive head of Columbia, Harry Cohn. The only studio head to model his office on that of Benito Mussolini, Cohn once convinced actor Paul Henreid to give up his valuable percentage in four films he had made for a subsidiary of Columbia by telling him that if he didn't, he would never make another picture in Hollywood for as long as he lived.

'Believe me, I can do it and I will,' Cohn said.

'Cohn,' wrote gossip columnist Hedda Hopper, 'was a man you had to stand in line to hate.'

Steiger added Louis B. Mayer's ability to turn on the tears when necessary. He had a grudging respect for such studio bosses. 'They were real sons of bitches,' he reflects. 'But I'd rather have them than some apparently good guy who will be nice to your face and then stab you in the back. The film business now is run by kids with computers.' Or kids who didn't even know that Steiger got an Oscar for *In the Heat of the Night*.

Jack Palance played the role of the actor driven to suicide. John Garfield had played the part when it was first staged in 1949, and his own life was later to mirror the events of the play.

Garfield's film career had been wrecked when Warner Brothers abandoned him after he appeared before the House Un-American Activities Committee. He was dead of a heart attack within a year of refusing to name names, and many people at the time thought he had killed himself.

Rod had trouble at first finding the motivation for his own character. He kept asking himself, What did Stanley Hoff want? What made him tick? What were his desires? What were his weaknesses?

He remembered something that he had been told by Vladimir Sokolov, the Russian-born character actor who had studied under Stanislavsky at the Moscow Arts Theatre. Stanislavsky had talked about the raisin in a bottle of kvass. Sometimes, he said, in looking at a part, you look for that raisin. If you can find the raisin in the bottle, the whole part in a way suddenly comes together.

Rod could not find the raisin in his role. So he decided to go to Saks Fifth Avenue in Beverly Hills and ask himself how Stanley Hoff would relate to the goods on display in the store:

> I went to women's perfume, and négligés, and the men's department and sports and I tried to figure out how, as Stanley, I felt about a baseball, how I felt about perfume. As I was going through the men's department I noticed these tie tacks, these little pins, fancy pins that keep your tie looking neat and pretty. And all of a sudden there was one that was in the shape of a tiny sterling silver question mark.
>
> And I said to myself, That's what he is, he's a question-mark man. He doubts his masculinity! That was because in the play his first big speech is about women. When the wife of the actor interrupts him, he says, 'What is a woman doing here?' And he says it with such disdain that I realized that this man had no respect for the feminine gender whatsoever.

Rod bought the tie tack, and wore it during the film, to remind himself that he had found the 'raisin'.

'I remember when I had to do that moment, I was trying to give myself the right feeling,' he says, 'and I thought of a time in London when at my then mother-in-law's house I had to take out the garbage can. When I took the lid off, it was full of maggots. It was disgusting. I said to myself, that's how Stanley feels about women; he thinks of them as maggots.'

He based Hoff's physical appearance on men he remembered from the New York Athletic Club – 'who came out in these black silk mohair suits, white shirts and beautiful suntan and silver hair'. But there was still a problem, and that was to get the audience to identify with such a demagogue. He had to find

100

some connection between them and Stanley, some weakness that would make him seem human. And he thought of a hearing aid.

Palance and Rod worked well together, even if their methods of preparing for their emotional and angry clashes were different. Between takes, while Palance did push-ups, Rod paced the set at a fast walk, pounding his hands together and talking to himself. 'This guy acts definitely nuts,' a veteran prop man remarked to a visiting journalist. There was tension between them. Palance, annoyed at Rod's attention-grabbing appearance in the film (white hair and a hearing-aid), and his barnstorming approach, threw some record albums at him after their first scene together. Aldrich had to pacify them both before they agreed to a truce. Steiger says this didn't happen, but Palance assured me that it did.

The best moment of the film, Rod thought, came as the result of a moment of improvisation by Palance, when they were arguing from different sides of the room. Rod turns his back to walk out. As he did so, he heard Palance running towards him.

I put my hands up because I thought he was going to kill me, I turned around, my arms crossed in front of my face, my eyes just above the top part of the cross, looking in his eyes, and then he did a wonderful thing; he just slapped me very lightly, with disgust. And it was such a put-down to Stanley Hoff. He dismissed him with this – not even a manly slap – more like you were hitting a mouldy, marshmallowy-type substance, and you didn't want to stick to it.

And it's those moments that are the narcotic of acting, the only high I love; because there is a chemical lift that's like a fresh wind that you first feel on a hot day, or unexpected laughter that somebody gives you, or the gift of love that comes out of nowhere. These highs last for one-hundredth of a second, that's how fast it goes, and the sad thing about it is, it dies at the moment you receive it, at the moment it's born, it dies. But that particular narcotic, which I love, the instinctive and intellectual discovery of something unprepared and unknown, and the living through it, is incredible.

Rod's characterization also benefited from an article he read in *Life* magazine about Treblinka. 'I thought, the people in this film are the people who run that. It was childish, but it worked for me.' Rod's performance was a definitive study of a bully and the film crackled with energy. As Pauline Kael remarked in the *New Yorker*, 'Who can take their eyes off the screen?' Rod's performance, she felt, was 'classic'.

Others had begun to take note of his acting. He topped the *Motion Picture Herald's* poll of exhibitors as the Star of Tomorrow, ahead of Jeffrey Hunter, Natalie Wood and Dana Wynter. More importantly, Fred Zinnemann called him one of the 'five most exciting actors in Hollywood', and Jerry Wald, the archetypal producer – he is said to be the original of Budd Schulberg's novel *What Makes Sammy Run?* – thought he was 'the most dynamic force since Cagney, the most promising newcomer since Brando'.

But unlike Brando or even Cagney, he was offered unsympathetic roles. His crooks had few saving graces. In 1958 he made a minor thriller, *Cry Terror*, for producer-director-screenwriter Andrew L. Stone, then venturing into ill-fated independent production with his wife Virginia, a writer and editor. Stone was a stickler for realism. This resulted in one unpleasant moment when the crew were filming on location in New York, in a tunnel beneath the Hudson River. Carbon-monoxide fumes from a generator used to power the lights caused twenty of the crew to become ill. Rod and Inger Stevens collapsed and she spent the night in hospital.

Stone took his script ideas from the pages of *Police Gazette* and filmed on location in New York, but the result still had a secondhand feel about it. Rod played a bespectacled, strung-out criminal mastermind who had planted a bomb on a plane with the reluctant help of a television repairman. Stone had improbably cast James Mason in this role, whose career at the time had collapsed in a welter of bad films.

Mason had been offered, and turned down, Rod's role. 'If I had been a little smarter I would have accepted since it was a much better part than that of the nice guy,' Mason said later. Even so, it was not the best of parts and offered Rod no challenges; it was one he had played before and would play again, as he well knew. His career, too, did not seem to be going anywhere very interesting, but at least he was the movie's main attraction, not merely a supporting actor.

The critics were lukewarm. 'James Mason, Rod Steiger and Inger Stevens appeared in it, but not noticeably for their own good,' wrote C. A. Lejeune in the *Observer*, though Dorothy Masters, of the *New York Daily News*, considered that Rod had been 'properly villainous in his role', while the *Herald Tribune*'s Paul Beckley thought he was 'superbly laconic'.

He was auditioned for the role as a business executive, starring with Judy Holliday in *Solid Gold Cadillac*, but the part eventually went to Paul Douglas. Instead, he was offered a meatier part in *The Harder They Fall*. While *Jubal* had been in CinemaScope and Technicolor, which Hollywood studios were using to tempt audiences back to the cinema and away from television, *The Harder They Fall*, like *The Big Knife*, was in black and white. It suited its gritty subject matter. Written by Philip Yordan from Budd Schulberg's novel, it exposed the seamier side of boxing and the crooked manipulations behind a heavyweight champion.

It was to become notable as Humphrey Bogart's last film. He played Eddie Willis, a sports reporter corrupted by Steiger's crooked entrepreneur Nick Benko, who promotes a third-rate Argentinian heavyweight, Toro Moreno, fixing his bouts so that he gains a reputation as a contender. Schulberg had based his novel partly on the career of the lumbering Italian Primo Carnera, a boxer built on a massive scale but lacking in genuine ability. Its Canadian-born director Mark Robson, a former editor with a talent for making commercially successful movies, worked with great skill, using among the cast some real heavyweight boxers such as Max Baer and Jersey Joe Walcott to provide a little authenticity.

Apart from the intrinsic interest of the film itself, there was the added fascination of watching the veteran champion Bogart going the distance with Rod, as their two acting styles clashed. A reporter from *Collier's* magazine noted their differences on the set, five minutes before Robson began shooting the film's drunk scene:

> As the other actors and actresses, including Humphrey Bogart, calmly received the usual eleventh-hour ministrations from eyebrow pencil and powder puff, an intense, heavy-set, villainous-looking actor was making some preparations of his own. First he beat his fist into the palm until bones cracked audibly. Then he ran ten stiff laps around the soundstage, stiff-arming imaginary opponents and pile-driving his knees like a college fullback with ninety-eight yards to go. He threw himself on the floor, did fifteen quick push-ups, sang eight roof-rocking bars of 'Celeste Aida', staggered to a nearby water cooler, sloshed water on his sweaty face until it dribbled down his chin, snarled tigerishly, then deliberately punched himself in the pit of the stomach. He paused to study the effect of these preparations in a mirror, then informed director Mark Robson that at last he was ready to perform.

Rod believed that you couldn't just jump into a scene. It was necessary to warm up, just as a boxer or a singer warmed up. 'Other actors kid my warm-up, but they don't kid the results,' he said.

Bogart hated the Method approach, calling it 'the scratch-your-ass-and-mumble school of acting'. But Rod was touched by the way that, when his close-ups were being shot, Bogart read his lines off-camera. No doubt he remembered how Brando had failed to provide such support during the making of *On the Waterfront*. In their scenes together, Bogart cleverly underplays his role the more Rod becomes emotionally involved; the contrast makes Rod's performance seem more florid than it actually is.

And the winner? The *Motion Picture Guide* thought it was Bogart; but critic Alan G. Barbour decided, 'Rather, it is Rod Steiger's portrayal of a thoroughly despicable man that garners our attention'. Rod came away from the film with great respect for Bogart, then dying from cancer which he concealed from his fellow workers. 'He had great authority,' he says.

Despite such excellent performances, Rod was still offered roles that gave him little opportunity, such as two films he made with director John Farrow. *Back From Eternity*, which Farrow had first made seventeen years earlier as *Five Came Back*, was the story of a plane crash in the Amazon jungle. It has not worn well, despite the presence of Robert Ryan and Anita Ekberg in the cast. *The Unholy Wife*, in which he starred opposite the pouting English actress Diana Dors, was a melodramatic mix of sex and death. This failed to work on-screen. Off-screen, Rod became friendly with his co-star, to the rage of her then-husband Dennis Hamilton, who demanded she return from Hollywood to England.

Rod went on to play the title role in *Al Capone*, directed by Richard Wilson, a long-time and long-suffering associate of Orson Welles, who was then on the staff of Universal Studios. It was to be Wilson's finest hour and forty-four minutes. It was also Rod's definitive performance of a megalomaniac – his bluster and bullying covering up for feelings of inadequacy. Elements of his Capone, dubbed by Chicago journalists 'the Napoleon of crime', turned up in later performances as Napoleon and as Mussolini.

Director and star were adamant that it wouldn't be a typical machine-gun movie. 'We have tried to point out that though a man may die, the evil he creates does not stop,' said Rod. He prepared himself for the role by reading the gangster's auto-biography. Then he went through the newspapers of the time, studying the reports of Capone's activities and his trial for income-tax evasion. As he read, he asked himself one question: what did Capone want? He decided that Capone wasn't so far removed from himself. The man wanted respect and recognition. 'He was, to me, a showman, an actor,' he told Helen Ross of the *New Yorker*.

For that reason, he decided his gestures in the part should be expansive. 'I wanted the man's natural actions to declare themselves,' he said. So he slung Capone's camel-hair coat across his shoulders and wore his hat at a jaunty angle and spoke in a roar. The performance hovered on the edge of caricature, but it worked brilliantly.

The film critic of the London *Times* was impressed: 'There is at times an over-reliance on mannerisms, on a broken incoherent manner of speech, on stylized gesture magnified by self-conscious photography, but the portrait is full length, that of an Iago consumed by megalomania, yet not without an inarticulate longing to be something other than he is. Nobody else has much chance against Mr Steiger.'

The early sixties did little to advance Rod's career. He appeared in a series of small and soon-forgotten movies, whose only saving grace seemed to be that they satisfied the restlessness that kept him moving around the world from one European country to another and then back to the States. His acting was not matched by the scripts or, often, the direction. But he kept working, at a furious rate.

He had dreams that were never, so far at least, to be realized: he wrote plays and scripts. One was about a father's uneasy relationship with his son that he hoped to produce, but he never managed to raise financial backing. He had another script, *The*

Untold Story, about an actor who cannot exist in the world of reality. It was based on his own experiences, and he planned to shoot it in Europe, possibly in Sicily or Sardinia, with the backing of an Italian production company, as a small but artistic black and white film. He longed to play a romantic lead, and vowed to lose weight; but he never became a slim actor and he came nearest to achieving this dream in a film, *Run of the Arrow*, that he regarded as 'terrible'. He hoped to play Othello, to Claire Bloom's Desdemona, but there never seemed to be a time when they were together long enough.

Casting directors typed him as a villain. Gossip columnist Louella Parsons dubbed him 'The Screen's No. 1 Bad Man', while the London *Evening News* described him as 'the man you would love to hate if you had the courage.' The London *Times*, hailing him as 'a very exciting film actor indeed,' found 'a strength in the square body and broad shoulders, and his method of attack suggests an odd amalgam of bull and cobra'.

The intensity of his acting seemed to work better in unheroic roles. Rod, also, had gained a certain reputation for awkwardness; he was not always the easiest actor to have on a set, regarding the script as only the skeleton of a film. 'Very few writers can write speech. In movies we haven't come close to life,' he says. 'It's always been glossed over with a kind of polish and a sense of false poetry.' He believed in rewriting, a sort of improvising that kept to the original thought but changed the words. Not everyone cared for his efforts, but his attitude remained constant: 'If you don't like what I'm doing, then replace me.' He had, he felt, earned the right to be left alone to do things his way. The directors he most enjoyed working with were those who left him most alone.

He was still ready to submit to the discipline of the Broadway stage, as he did when he played the outlaw in *Rashomon* in 1959, though his demands and expectations remained high. 'I think theatre should be a place where you can see things that you can't see on television or at the movies,' he says. 'When we get ourselves down to a common denominator that is truly common, art gets in trouble. Everything today is calculated towards the feelings, not towards the mind. I believe in instincts first and intellect second, but an actor must have some intellectual training because when his instincts don't work, he needs some technical things to help him.'

Rashomon was a costly production, budgeted at $150,000, a large amount for a work that was not a musical. Sets were by leading British designer Oliver Messel and featured a rainstorm and a green bamboo jungle on a turntable. The cast included two scene-stealing actors, Akim Tamiroff and Oscar Homolka, as well as Claire Bloom.

Kurosawa's film was a hard act to follow, with its depiction of the different ways four people view terrible events at the Rashomon Gate in Kyoto a thousand years ago: the rape of a bride and the murder of her husband, a samurai. Three – a bandit, the wife, and the ghost of her husband – are intent on justifying their behaviour; the fourth, a woodcutter who has no axe to grind, tells a different story. The New York critics were enthusiastic, although those in Philadelphia, where the play had previewed the previous month, had been more divided in their responses.

For the *New York Post*'s Richard Watt Jr, though, it was Oscar Homolka and Claire Bloom, ranging 'from innocent victim to conniving little slut', who took the acting honours. Brooks Atkinson of the *New York Times* considered that the leading performances were all extraordinary; Kenneth Tynan concurred in the *New Yorker*, 'Nothing on Broadway is better acted', while, in the *Daily Mirror*, Robert Coleman found Rod's performance as the bandit 'magnificently animalish'.

Rod's role, like that of Noel Willman as the samurai and Claire as his wife, needed a virtuoso performance, since each version of the crime required a change in their characterization. Also, for Rod, it involved a precisely choreographed sword fight with Willman, their blades clashing in an intricate ballet. Originally wooden weapons were to be used, but they did not make the right sound, so potentially lethal steel swords were substituted, leading gossip columnists to write that Rod had increased his life insurance as a result.

It was, perhaps, typical of his luck that when, in 1963, MGM decided to film a version of *Rashomon* in an American setting as *The Outrage*, the studio signed Claire as the violated woman but not Rod as her violator. The role of bandit went to Paul Newman instead. 'He's a good-looking boy and he's bigger at the box office. It's as simple as that,' said Rod, but it was still hurtful. Martin Ritt's direction, though, failed to overcome the repetitious nature of the oft-told tale, and the film flopped.

Rod returned again to the Broadway stage in 1962 in a revival of Orson Welles' *Moby Dick Rehearsed*, a play Welles had written seven years earlier to give himself a plum role as both Melville's hero Captain Ahab and a nineteenth-century barnstorming actor-manager. Welles had opened it in London with a cast that also included the young Joan Plowright, where it ran for four weeks to critical approval, though the audiences seemed bewildered. Douglas Campbell directed Rod in Welles' role, but the play was liked neither by critics nor audience and ran for twelve performances.

But Steiger was beginning to find Broadway no more appealing than Hollywood. 'There was a time when actors returned to the stage for a stretching out, a cleansing,' he said. 'That isn't true any more. The best acting is more likely to be found in films. And Broadway is becoming more like the stockmarket. It's only interested in making money.' He did plan one more foray into stage acting, signing to play the role of Bertolt Brecht's *Galileo* at the Lincoln Center Repertory Company in April 1967. But when the time came, he was too ill to take on the part and the production was cancelled.

Steiger was one American actor prepared to turn his back on his homeland and find roles that would satisfy him. In 1962 he made a French-German-Italian co-production *On Friday at Eleven* (*An einem Freitag um halb zwelf*), directed by Alvin Rakoff. The film was based on James Hadley Chase's thriller about a gang planning to rob a heavily armoured American army truck, in which he starred with Nadja Tiller, Peter van Eyck and Ian Bannen.

Then came another British film. Guy Green's *The Mark* was a worthy, serious drama about a sexual psychopath, a child abuser, haunted by his past. Rod's performance as psychiatrist Dr McNally was good, but it was Stuart Whitman who received an Academy award nomination as the abuser. Rod then joined the vast cast of stars providing cameo performances in *The Longest Day* as the commander of a destroyer during the Normandy invasions.

It was followed by *Reprieve*, also known as *Convicts Four*, about a murderer saved from the electric chair, who becomes a painter. Based on the autobiography of John Resko and starring Ben Gazzara, it never found a consistent tone under the first-and-only-time direction of screenwriter Millard Kaufman, and it was not helped by a series of cameo performances from, among others, Sammy Davis Jr, Vincent Price, Ray Walston and Broderick Crawford.

Rod played a detective-sergeant in *13 West Street* (also known as *The Tiger Among Us* and, confusingly, *13 East Street*) from Leigh Brackett's novel about an engineer's struggle with a gang of hoodlums. Alan Ladd starred and Philip Leacock directed.

In 1963, Steiger went to Italy to make three films with three of the country's leading directors. By Hollywood working standards (early morning starts), the movies were something of a rest cure. Filming began at around eleven in the morning, stopping for a leisurely lunch and then resuming at around four in the afternoon for a further four hours.

Hands Over the City (*Le Mani sulla Città*), dealing with exploitation in the Neapolitan building industry, was directed by the neo-realist Neapolitan Francesco Rosi, who had learned his craft in the late forties and early fifties working as an assistant on Luchino Visconti's first ground-breaking films. He was lucky enough to have a considerable private income, because his wife owned a string of boutiques in Rome. Rosi approached Rod after seeing him in *On the Waterfront* and *The Big Knife*, deciding that his performances had the sort of power he needed for the film. At the time, there was no script, but after Rosi explained what he wanted to do, Rod agreed to appear.

Rosi, in common with other neo-realist directors, liked to use non-professional actors. 'It is odd,' he commented after making the film, 'because Steiger, who is a very professional actor, worked face to face in direct sound with Guido Alberti, a non-professional, yet their performances blended together very well.'

Like Rosi's other politically committed films, *Hands Over the City* was based on actual happenings, investigating the corruption of power and relationships between crime and the state, but for all its quality it was judged too parochial to receive wide distribution outside Italy.

Gli Indifferenti, otherwise *Time of Indifference*, was written and directed by Francesco Maselli, a prodigy who had made his first film in his early twenties, but who, ten years later, was beginning to lose his reputation. It was based on Alberto Moravia's novel about the rise of fascism. Rod played a financier who transferred his affections from his mistress (Paulette Goddard) to her daughter (Claudia Cardinale), with Shelley Winters as a former mistress, busily seducing Tomas Milian. Shelley Winters reported that filming 'started in chaos and ended up in shambles'.

Rod gave a powerful performance, but the problem was that Maselli and his influential producer, Franco Cristaldi, were at loggerheads, one attempting to make a political film, the other insisting on emphasizing the erotic subplot and his current girl-friend, Claudia Cardinale. Filming wasn't helped by the fact that Maselli's English was virtually non-existent. The cast spoke the lines in their own languages, so that the dialogue on set was mainly a mixture of English and the Spanish of Cuban-born Milian. Cardinale, remembered Winters, 'just made sounds'. As was common practice in Italy, the film was to be dubbed later, according to where it managed to get released.

It took two years to reach the United States. When Steiger was called to a studio to dub his role for the American version, it was discovered that the film's original soundtrack was missing from the print. There was no script available either. A lip reader had to be summoned to reconstruct the dialogue before he and the others could record it. The effort was hardly worth it. Audiences stayed away and critic Judith Crist characterized it as 'warmed-over-weltschmerz minestrone'. It proved, she added, 'that when all roads lead actors to Rome they don't give a damn what they do once they get there'.

Ermanno Olmi's *Man Named John*, also known as *And There Came a Man* (*E venne un Uomo*), was a study of Pope John XXIII, in which Rod appeared as a narrator and as the pontiff's alter ego. It was a departure for Olmi, who until then had always used ordinary people in his films, bringing in professional actors (with many regrets) only at the dubbing stage, since he felt that otherwise he could not convey the truth of a situation. 'Actors are followed by the public not for the characters they represent on the screen but because the actors themselves are a model of success in our society,' he said.

Man Named John mixed documentary footage with scenes of Rod in dramatic interludes, although in all of them he remains himself, never wearing ecclesiastical garments. The device was a clumsy one and the film never came to life. Olmi blamed himself. 'It was not Steiger's fault. It was mine. How I hate myself for making a mess of that film,' he said afterwards. 'Maybe I was intimidated by the greatness of Pope John.'

Rod returned to television to act with Claire Bloom as the doomed medieval couple Abelard and Heloise in *Dark Lover* by Arthur W. Rubin. But that was no more than marking time, and he knew it. Television was no longer an arena for challenge; the programmes came and went and single plays no longer forced themselves on public consciousness, as *Marty* had.

S teiger has always believed that he is more appreciated in Europe than in America. It was the British who, in 1957, gave Rod his first respite from conventionally 'heavy' roles. He came to London to make *Across the Bridge*, directed by Ken Annakin and adapted from Graham Greene's short story. A shady English financier gets stuck in a small Mexican town while two detectives attempt to lure him back over the border to the USA with the aid of his only friend, a dog. Greene approved Guy Elmes' script which added many complications to the original, changing the hero into a millionaire living in New York who, fleeing on a train, takes the identity of a Mexican he pushes out of the carriage, only to discover that the Mexican was also a hunted man. It was Elmes who wanted Rod for the role. But when he first suggested it, the reply was, 'Who's Rod Steiger?', which suggests that the British were out of touch with American films.

Annakin felt that there would be a clash of styles between Rod and the English actors Bernard Lee and David Knight. But Rod spent a fortnight in London without pay, working with Annakin before shooting began and wondering how not to be upstaged by a dog.

'I've never known an actor put so much thought and preparation into a performance,' Annakin told the *Daily Mail*.

At times he overdid it, and we had some tense moments on the floor. For the first week of filming things were touch and go between us. There was one especially trying day when he found nothing right with the script or the other performances. He decided that British scriptwriters knew nothing about dialogue and seemed to think all British actors were savages. I let him go on airing his Method jargon but the next day I put my foot down. It came home to him then that the British did know something about acting after all.

'Bullshit!' says Steiger. He remembers their collaboration in different terms: 'I had arguments and differences with Ken Annakin. We cut and rewrote the script together. We changed a lot of other things, but that's the way I work.'

It was during this film that I first met Steiger and it seems to me that the argument for control of the film was entirely his, even to the extent of suggesting camera angles. The other actors, too, seemed to take their cue from him, asking him which way they should play a scene. Of course, I might have been mistaken, glancing in on the situation from the wrong aspect, but from what I saw, Steiger could almost have asked for a co-directing credit. My opinion is that Annakin was far too pleasant a man to really put his foot down; a craftsman of some repute in British studios, he mattered little at all in Steiger's scheme of things.

This was a time, in British movies, when American stars who were on the downhill path came over to London to add fading lustre to cheap movies. I remember one wonderful alcoholic star who brought his own male nurse with him to stop his drinking. But Steiger was not on the skids, and was totally sure of himself and of the upward path he was climbing.

Part of the problem was the English attitude towards Method acting, perhaps best summed up by Leonard Mosley's hyperbolic appreciation of Rod's approach in the *Daily Express*: 'He mouths, he weeps, he grovels, splutters, shudders, grunts and moans his way through the script. Then, with the help of a strong-minded editor, he cuts out the surplus nonsense and shapes from the rest a true picture of the character he is attempting to portray.'

115

Annakin was happy with the finished film, regarding it as his best work, but it was not a commercial success. 'It would be easy to say that Rod Steiger was not a big enough star name to bring people into the cinema. But on the other hand it wouldn't have been *Across the Bridge* without Rod,' he said.

'Actors have the myth that it is ruinous to do a scene with a dog or a baby,' said Rod. 'When I told my Hollywood friends that I was making a picture called *Across the Bridge*, they all said, "You're through, finished. You're doing a picture with a dog." I told them, "I don't understand what you're saying. Where the dog is important we'll photograph the dog. Where I'm important, we'll photograph me." That's what we did, and the dog and I both came out alive.'

It was a film for Rod to write home about. And his letter could easily have read: 'Dear Hollywood, You never treated me this well.' The film, I wrote in my *Picturegoer* review, put him firmly on the bandwagon reserved for star quality. It was a superb one-man-band affair, conducted with harsh integrity. Rod forcefully crossed the bridge between Method, mannerism and top-line performance. Like a pinned butterfly, one's attention was transfixed by his acting. Rod, too, felt that he had finally made his mark. Now, he thought, I'll be offered better scripts. The reality was different, even though *Newsweek* referred to him as 'another Paul Muni'. During a talk at Filmstage, a film workshop, Rod said,

Did I know that we were going into a period when there would be no better scripts? Did I know that it was comedy time? And I am not exactly the world's greatest comedian. I had great offers. Would I like to play Elvis Presley's manager? I said, 'After twenty years as an actor, I will not play Elvis Presley's manager. It would kill me.' Nothing against Mr Presley, but I was really hurt. So I started to turn things down.

I had to wait two years for a decent script. And while I was waiting, I went into debt for fourteen thousand dollars. I was supposed to be an international name, but I was sent one bad script after another.

He turned back to television, appearing in June 1958 on television's *Playhouse 90* in Rod Serling's *A Town Has Turned to Dust*, directed by John Frankenheimer, in which he played a weak sheriff confronting a mob led by shopkeeper William Shatner (later to become Captain Kirk in *Star Trek*), determined to lynch a Mexican boy accused of robbing his store. *Variety* was impressed: 'It was a difficult role and he caught every nuance of the tortured law enforcement officer with rare perception,' and it brought a telegram from star actor Paul Muni – 'Bless you for a wonderful performance' – that he framed and hung on his wall.

Halfway through the sixties everything suddenly became right for him – he was matched with a good script and a director at the height of his powers. First there was *The Pawnbroker*, directed by Sidney Lumet, with Rod in the title role as Sol Nazerman, survivor of a Nazi concentration camp in which his wife and children died, who runs a Harlem pawnshop as a front for a local gangster.

Rod still regards it as his finest performance, one that he was happy to take despite the fact that he was paid only fifty thousand dollars, well below his going rate. Lumet was a director he trusted; they had first worked together on the television series *You Are There*. But *The Pawnbroker's* excellence counted for little at first in the market-place.

Its producer Ely Landau had problems getting it screened. Every major US distributor rejected it as a movie that no audience would want to see. One executive told him that it would never earn back its costs. So Landau distributed it himself, with two small companies, Allied Artists and American International, taking over at a later date. In Britain, the reaction was the same. When the major distributors rejected it, Landau arranged for it to be shown at an independent West End cinema. It was only when the film had run for fourteen weeks there that the Rank organization agreed to distribute it. (Three years after its initial

117

release, the film had earned around $5m in rentals around the world and Landau anticipated that it would eventually take $8m, giving him a profit of $5m.)

Critic Judith Crist wrote that it was technically a 'little film' because of its budget of £1.25m and its star, 'Rod Steiger, a brilliant and bravura actor whose performances in *On the Waterfront* and *The Big Knife* are unforgettable but who, of course, just doesn't rank at the box office the way a Rock Hudson or a Heston does.'

She felt that although the film was remarkable, it fell short of greatness. 'It is distinguished not only by Mr Steiger's portrayal of a man encased in the world's anguish but also by several other performers and, above all, perhaps, by its dealing with its story on its own terms.'

Pauline Kael in the *New Yorker*, on the other hand, thought it a terrible movie, though she added, 'Rod Steiger's power makes our questioning of much of the action seem like quibbling.' When it reached London in October 1966, the *Daily Mail* critic, Cecil Wilson, wrote that Rod's performance 'seems to encompass all the agony ever inflicted on man'.

Rod was living in London when he got the news that his performance had earned him an Oscar nomination as best actor. Apart from his house on the beach at Malibu, he, Claire and Anna moved between four homes, including an apartment in Brooklyn and a cottage in Ireland, not far from John Huston's sprawling home in County Galway.

He returned to Hollywood for the ceremony, expecting to win. The nominations included one other American, the sometimes surly Lee Marvin (who did not suffer journalists gladly unless, like me, you could match him drink for drink) for his twin roles in the comic western *Cat Ballou*. There were also two Britons, Richard Burton for *The Spy Who Came in From the Cold* and Laurence Olivier for *Othello*, and an Austrian, Oskar Werner, for *Ship of Fools*. Not only did Rod feel that he had given the best performance of his career, but the press was on his side. 'I want

Rod to get that Oscar,' gushed Wanda Hale in the *New York Daily News*. 'There is no finer actor in this country or any other. He is an American and I am patriotic.'

Rod was in no doubt that the prize would be his. At the ceremony he found himself sitting behind Marvin, but he was certain that Marvin was a no-hoper. What chance had a slight, comic picture like *Cat Ballou* over *The Pawnbroker*, which had such social significance? He remembers thinking, Rod, my boy, you're going to win.

As he heard the words, 'And the winner is . . .', he began to button his jacket and try to decide whether he should saunter down the aisle, run down, or kiss a few people on the way. Then he heard '. . . Lee Marvin!'

'I was absolutely shocked,' says Rod. 'And Lee Marvin walked up and got a prize he probably and justly deserved, and I got a spanking from the forces of nature which said, "Listen, jackass, never take happiness, never take your talent, for granted. Never, in any walk of life, take for granted your capabilities. Each minute a second of life is a challenge – so sit still, schmuck, and let this be a lesson to you. Happiness has to be earned and respected. Rewards must never be taken for granted." I never forgot that moment.'

The Pawnbroker, too, is not something easily forgotten. It is about a kind of redemption, with the pawnbroker earning a living in downtown New York and trying to forget the memories which have destroyed his life. Not even a black girl bearing her breasts at him, as a method of persuasion, can impinge on the morally calloused shell that life has thickened around him. It is, for me, perhaps the most important movie in Steiger's career, after *On the Waterfront*. It is, also, one of the least flamboyant – perhaps because Lumet was a much more imposing director than Annakin. In fact, Lumet told me: 'Sure Rod has weaknesses of rhetoric, but you talk them through with him. I explained that this solitary Jew could not rise to heights of emotion; he had been hammered by life and by people. The faith he had to find was in other people, because God had betrayed him.'

Even then, though, the Jew's redemption is not complete. It is the artistic weight of the idea that it is only the light at the end of the tunnel that he glimpses in the shooting of someone he has come to care for. And it is that backing off from complete tragic articulacy that brings tears to my eyes every time I see the film.

A chance to use his comedy talents came in Tony Richardson's eccentrically lavish production of Evelyn Waugh's small but deadly satire on Hollywood, the British Empire and the American way of death in *The Loved One*. Many writers, including Luis Buñuel and Elaine May, had tried to turn the novella into a film, without success. Much to Waugh's alarm, Terry Southern and Christopher Isherwood had updated the original in flamboyant style. The cast gathered around the two young lovers of Robert Morse and Anjanette Comer was an extraordinary one, ranging from Sir John Gielgud, who based his performance on Cecil Beaton, to Milton Berle and Liberace.

Although the role of Mr Joyboy was written as a homosexual, Rod played him as a eunuch instead. Rod based his curly-haired appearance on a bust of Apollo he saw on the way to meet Tony Richardson and asked if he could copy it. Richardson agreed enthusiastically. Rod improvised another scene of him answering the phone by suggesting to Richardson that they find a novel method of doing it. They decided to do it by using some barbells that were background props. As he played the scene, Rod discovered that the barbells were extremely weighty and that in normal circumstances he could never have lifted them. 'When I did get home that night after finishing the scene, my wife took one look at me and asked me what was the matter. I said, "We answered the phone a different way".'

Despite being an enjoyable experience, the finished film was a mess, hampered by disagreements between Richardson and his cinematographer, Haskell Wexler, during filming, and

Richardson's clashes with its editors after. But it was often amusing, including Rod's turn as Mr Joyboy, a masterly embalmer whose work reflects his feelings: his corpses smile when he is in love, frown when he loses his love.

Bosley Crowther in the *New York Times* found it offensive, 'but for reasons other than the boldness and indelicacy of its theme, or, indeed for the many insensitive and impious things it shows'. He found Rod 'appropriately repulsive as the hideously epicene Mr Joyboy'.

Rod next had a chance to display his considerable skills with characterizations and accents in *No Way to Treat a Lady*, a black comedy about a serial killer, which was to meet with a mixed response. It was a sort of American variation on *Kind Hearts and Coronets*, trying for a similar elegant wit in dealing with death and giving Rod the opportunity to emulate Alec Guinness by playing half a dozen roles, as his killer dons various disguises.

As an example of how Steiger could draw art from life there is an ad-libbed line which has become a by-word in our household. Steiger has occasion to try to placate one of the lonely old ladies whom he might well slaughter. But the lady in question is a tough old bird, accusing him of being a homosexual. Realizing that he is scuppered, Steiger withdraws from the scene, throwing over his shoulder the words, 'Doesn't mean to say you're not a nice person!'

I have seen the film half a dozen times and that line always gets a laugh. It's a throwaway that boomerangs back. And it came from a friend of Rod's. 'I heard it once and thought there had to come an occasion when it would fit. Sure enough it came during *No Way to Treat a Lady*.'

Many critics praised his performance. In the *Observer*, Tom Milne was impressed: 'He gives a virtuoso display of characterization and comic timing which all but turns a minor black comedy into a masterpiece.' Others were dismissive. Andrew Sarris in the *Village Voice* thought 'his characterization is buried under a pile of soggy ham'.

Pauline Kael's review in the *New Yorker* was even harsher: 'I've never seen Steiger so bad, so uninventively, ordinary bad as he is in his undisguised role in this movie, and he's only a little better in his disguises, acting high on the hog.' She complained that the film did nothing but 'give Steiger a chance to show off his comic accents. And considering how good he was in roles like the Irish psychiatrist in *The Mark* and the Southern chief of police in *In the Heat of the Night*, he's surprisingly crude – no better than his material.'

Rod followed that with a role in *Dr Zhivago*, David Lean's film that, as John Simon put it, 'does for snow what his Lawrence of Arabia did for sand'. Lean simplified Boris Pasternak's sprawling novel of the Russian revolution into a story of a man who is married to one woman and in love with another. 'The trick was in not having the audience condemn the lovers,' he said.

Lean wanted Marlon Brando as Victor Komarovsky, the dapper, grasping lawyer whom Lara (Julie Christie) tries to kill, horrified by his attempt to seduce her as well as her mother. He wrote to Brando, but after waiting a month for a reply, he offered the role to James Mason, who agreed by return, signing his letter of acceptance, 'Elatedly, James'.

In his casting notes for the film, Lean wrote that he needed an actor who had 'enough dexterity and personality to convince an audience that he could not only weather the revolution (changing sides as he does) but that he could end up as Minister of Justice. He must be old enough to make his seduction of the schoolgirl, Lara, shocking, and not attractive enough to be in any logical sense a rival to Zhivago.' He worried that Mason had overtones of a 'dark, dreaming Svengali', but thought he was a good enough actor to overcome the problem. When Mason dropped out, Rod accepted the role gladly.

Nic Roeg, who was the cinematographer, before being replaced by Lean's usual lighting cameraman, Freddie Young, remembers Rod arriving in Madrid and going to the caravan where Lean was holding court and fighting off arguments in a tense atmosphere. 'What's the matter?' said Rod. 'Somebody's father just died?' Only Roeg laughed.

Lean was a slow worker, and Rod was to spend six restless months in Madrid. 'I don't like bullfighting, I can't stand flamenco and I can't eat fish; Madrid is a lot like Chicago – awful.' Once again he was cast as a villain, though he would dispute that description.

'People say Komarovsky was such a mean man. I say, what did he do? He slept with the mother and daughter. Most of the men in the world would give their right arm to sleep with two women – the mother and daughter. He came back and tried to save them both. His mistake was that he thought Lara was another one night stand and he fell in love with her. He wasn't a bad person.'

Rod still carried with him the reputation of being difficult to work with, though Lean, too, was known as a hard taskmaster, a man with little sympathy for, and sometimes downright cruelty towards, actors. Added to his natural arrogance was the fact that his deal with MGM made him the highest paid director in the business. (After working for more than a year on Lean's *Ryan's Daughter*, its American star Christopher Jones abandoned acting altogether.) When Rod had dinner with Lean a couple of days after beginning work, Lean told him, 'I'm glad you're here. You know, they told me to watch out Monday morning "because Mr Steiger is coming".' Rod replied, 'They told me to watch out on Monday because "you're going to meet David Lean".'

As a film it was dated almost as soon as it was made, because its vast romanticism was going out of fashion. That did not stop it from making a lot of money at the box office, but looked at now it is very unsatisfactory; as though the union of two errant lovers was more important than the epic political events that are their context. David Lean had captured the sweep of a nation's convulsions, but ground them down to make a small chaff for a tedious affair. There are many who consider Lara a bit of a spoilsport not to have fallen completely for the villain who seduced her.

Omar Sharif seemed much too 'holily oily' for our complete identification. He brought something 'powerful, many-sided and sexual to the role', wrote Pauline Kael. But it was Tom Courtenay, in the role of a student turned revolutionary, who was nominated for an Academy award as best supporting actor.

Looking back at the year at the end of 1965, Judith Crist celebrated what she called 'nonstars' – actors who were exciting to watch without reaching stardom – Lee Marvin, Harry Andrews, Richard Attenborough and Dirk Bogarde. Rod was among them. 'Can you keep your attention from Rod Steiger, whatever the scene?' she wrote. 'There is a sense of completeness in each of his portraits, major or minor, from his cringing triumph as the producer in *The Big Knife* to the groping, untidy psychiatrist in *The Mark* to the searing excesses of *The Pawnbroker* and the very high camp of *The Loved One*.'

His next role was something of a star turn, as a repressed homosexual in *The Sergeant*, but it failed to satisfy Pauline Kael. She wrote; 'If Steiger had grabbed the boy he loves and been rebuffed an hour and a half earlier, he could have said, "All right, so I made a mistake", and maybe the picture could have gone on and been *about* something.'

She added:

Wasn't the idea behind the financing of the movie that the star must be an actor the public likes and thinks is a great *actor*, so they know it's not for real? Why else would Rod Steiger be cast in the lead? A repressed (if that's what it's meant to be) homosexual seems to be totally outside his range; he keeps his face prissy, with his lips pursed, throughout the movie, as if waiting for his emotional outbursts, so that he can let go, but the prissy blank is a blank. Does playing a homosexual paralyse him as an actor?

Rod agreed that the film did not come off, though the idea had been good and the execution fair. In his talk at Filmstage, Rod explained his attitude to film acting:

Films are a business all right, but I've always tried to avoid business – although I've found that the more successful an actor gets, the more he comes to sound like a businessman.

To the business people in films, actors are a commodity, a product. As an actor, you are considered to be a can of peas. OK. But you have the right to be the best goddamn can of peas that ever walked. You have the right to work so hard that the business people have to listen to you. You have the personal obligation to yourself to make yourself the best product possible according to your own terms. Not the biggest or the most successful, but the best quality.

He stressed the importance of actors doing their homework, of not taking their talent for granted. He added that the best judge of an actor's performance was the actor. 'He is the only one who knows when he's really cheating. Something inside of him tells him, unless he is such an egomaniac that he thinks that anything he does is marvellous. But in that case, he's dead anyway, and it doesn't really make any difference.'

Rod recalled something that Charlie Chaplin once told him – 'I'm not an actor, my boy, I'm a poet.' The actor, he felt, had to be some kind of poet, had to maintain an idealism if he was to survive as a human being.

Then came one of those mistakes he half regrets, is half proud of. He was offered the title role in *Patton*. But after reading the script he turned it down. 'I will not glorify war,' he told the producers. 'What a schmuck I was, an idiot,' he says now. 'It was the biggest business mistake of my life. If my *Patton* had been half as good as George C. Scott's, I might have got to do *The Godfather* . . . It set my career back.'

*　　*　　*

One of Steiger's finest moments was a role that combined his threatening presence with an underlying sensitivity, as the beleaguered sheriff in *In the Heat of the Night*. Judith Crist, including it among her top ten films of 1967, wrote:

> What is remarkable is Rod Steiger's subtle delineation of a hitherto clichéd character, the authority with which he moulds the many moods of a stolid man and the rhythm of his playing against Sidney Poitier's established noble-Negro character. But under Norman Jewison's knowing and at times beautiful direction, Poitier brings new facets to his characterization. The film, however, is Steiger's all the way.

In the *New Yorker*, Pauline Kael noted Rod's 'comic performance that was even funnier for being so unexpected – not only from Steiger's career which had been going in other directions, but after the apparently serious opening of the film.' In *Life* magazine, Richard Schickel praised 'a wonderful piece of acting – humorous, shrewd and strong without being domineering or self-admiring'.

Roger Ebert had been struck by a scene in a warehouse, where Rod's police chief confronts four hoodlums who are attacking Sidney Poitier, grabbing the ringleader by the shirt, pulling him close and swiftly slapping him three times. 'When Steiger does this,' he wrote, 'a low-pitched exasperated moan escapes from his lips. It is this moan that is so chilling. I've never heard anything like it before, from Steiger or anyone else. It is a moan of venomous hatred and loathing. It could not possibly have been in the script. It came from somewhere inside Steiger.'

Ebert felt that this skill to disappear into his characters had limited Rod's success: moviegoers did not come to see him because they never knew whether they would be able to recognize him.

Rod, having earlier missed out on an Oscar for his performance in *The Pawnbroker*, was not hopeful when he was nominated as best actor. This time around, Rod was up against tough opposition: an all-American group of Paul Newman for *Cool Hand Luke*, Dustin Hoffman for *The Graduate*, Warren Beatty for *Bonnie and Clyde* and Spencer Tracy for *Guess Who's Coming to Dinner?*

But *In the Heat of the Night* triumphed, winning five Oscars and becoming the first detective film to get an Academy award for best film. Rod carried off the prize as best actor. Looking back on the twenty-seven films he had made up to that point, he considered that a satisfying proportion, around twenty, were creditable, even if there had been some he would like to have seen buried.

In the Heat of the Night was to be a watershed in Steiger's career. For good or bad he is still not sure.

That he deserved an Oscar is undoubtedly true. There is one speech he makes when he, as the sheriff, and Poitier as the detective, drink through the night and Steiger's character slowly reveals his own frustration and hurts. It is a phenomenal scene, exposing the truth of the man by a slow peeling off of layers of the armour that all human beings take on through their lives. 'We got through a bottle of whisky,' says Steiger, 'Mr Poitier and I. It was a wonderful kick-start to a most difficult character who was reticent to the point of hiding out in himself.' That kind of sanctuary Rod Steiger has never sought.

PART THREE

IN THE FORESTS OF THE NIGHT

– 8 –

The 1970s were to prove to be a bad time professionally for Steiger. Not only were Hollywood producers not offering the extraordinary roles he needed, but even the chances for star turns were limited. He was finding it difficult to escape from typecasting as a Mafia heavy or a near-psychopath – roles which he could invest with great menace but again limited his opportunities to display his skill. Often, the parts were paper-thin, hardly written, relying on his ability to add some individuality.

He remembered how bad he had felt when he found himself in debt. He vowed it would not happen again. 'I find a part I can do without losing my self-respect and do it, while I wait and hope for better things,' he said. He had also learned another lesson. That in films, you have power only if you are expensive.

As a consequence he spent much time in Europe, looking and hoping for more challenging opportunities. But even there, although he worked with several leading directors, the projects turned out to be among their less successful, or were so local in their interest that they hardly travelled elsewhere, doing little for his reputation.

He spent five months in the Ukraine, playing Napoleon in *Waterloo*, a Russian-Italian co-production directed by Sergei Bondarchuk. It was not an altogether happy experience. Bondarchuk's English, he noted, was limited to 'How are you?' and 'I come back soon'. In French, he could manage only *'Bonjour'*. When Rod reluctantly got astride a horse that had been described as very gentle, it promptly bolted after a nearby explosion. For his close-ups, they put him in the saddle on a saw-horse, which was the sort of horse he liked.

He read biographies of Napoleon as part of his research, trying to find some clue to the man's character. 'Napoleon was sick, tired and lonely. I've been all those things so I can understand them. That was all I had to go on,' he said. He was to find the key he needed in the report on Napoleon's autopsy. 'Here was a man whose mind was growing and his body dying at the same time,' which was a line he added to the script in a voice-over, as Napoleon sits by the fireside contemplating his bleak future.

There was one frustrating moment, in which Rod was delivering a long speech to camera – or, rather, the five cameras that Bondarchuk had set up. The scene was going well; Rod could feel the tingling sensation that signalled a moment of transcendence, one of those rare occasions when an actor surpasses himself. It was just then that Bondarchuk shouted, 'Cut!'

The cameras had run out of film; the producers had been cutting costs by using short ends, pieces of film left over from longer reels and sold off cheaply. Rod burst into tears. 'You don't understand. This is not a job to me,' he cried. 'This is my life!' Bondarchuk decided then and there that Rod was more Russian than he was.

The film exists in a four-hour Russian version, but the one that reached the West had been heavily edited, much to Rod's distress, and lasted for a little under two-and-a-quarter hours, culminating in an hour-long battle sequence. Nevertheless, *Variety* found Steiger's portrayal remarkably powerful: 'It's a Method performance, with his sudden blazes of rage highlighting his moody introspection.' But the English critical journal *Monthly Film Bulletin* found 'the alternation of choked Method whisper and deadpan peremptoriness, presumably meant to differentiate the private and public Napoleons, soon grow remarkably wearisome.' (Some time later, a man came up to Rod and told him he knew Napoleon and the Emperor wasn't at all like Rod's version!)

True to type or not, Steiger's performance was, as I wrote, one of the few that could upstage a battlefield.

There was a royal première for *Waterloo*, one of those occasions which prove to the movie-makers that what they have achieved is worthy of such regal spectacle. In this case the Queen was attending and the stars were lined up to pay honour and homage from one kind of showbusiness to another.

Steiger had planned to bring a beautiful black girl, Marpessa Dawn, star of the film *Black Orpheus*, but her nerve ran out at the thought of all that noble glitz. She rang Steiger to say she couldn't make it.

So he waited alone, uneasily in line, to press the royal flesh. There was a ripple of anticipation: 'She's coming, she's arrived, she's HERE!' And there, indeed, she was, clasping his hand as though she would never let go and talking the small talk that is expected on such a walkabout.

'What a vast movie!' she chimed. 'A huge epic!'

Steiger was, for him, tongue-tied. Then he said the first thing that came into his head. Certainly it wasn't as sparkling as the tiara that clasped the royal brow, but it came from the heart.

'I don't know how they put the bloody thing together,' he said.

It was the word 'bloody' that did it. As though a mouse had suddenly appeared under her balldress she jumped a little and then moved swiftly on. Her aide shot Steiger a reproachful glance at putting the Queen through such a grievous experience.

Steiger was not daunted. After all it had been the kind of ad-lib by which he made his living.

Steiger's meetings with majesty have often been more cordial. He was mightily impressed by President Clinton, so much so that he had a small Oscar made after one of Clinton's speeches to Congress. 'I thought he had tremendous presence.'

A presidential secretary wrote to say that Clinton was deeply touched and when their paths crossed, Rod Steiger handed over the 'Oscar'.

Bill Clinton said he was honoured. So was Steiger.

Steiger is always aware of the dignity of the performer, even when up against the demands of royalty. He and the singer Tony Bennett came to London to appear in a charity performance sponsored by Princess Margaret. They were invited back to Princess Margaret's home.

'I realized, though, that they were taking advantage of Tony. He had to keep on singing songs, and not just his famous "I Left My Heart In San Francisco". He looked tired; after all he had been singing all night. He was being treated as an unpaid entertainer and not an honoured guest.

'So I said to Princess Margaret that Tony had an early rehearsal next day and should be in bed. She looked very miffed, but agreed.

'Outside, Tony said, "Thank Christ. And thank you. I didn't know how to get out of that. And I was dropping."'

For Steiger, entertainers are not performing seals – or slaves.

After *Waterloo*, in a similar vein, a sort of halfway house between Capone and Napoleon, he starred in the left-wing director Carlo Lizzani's *Last Days of Mussolini* (*Mussolini: Ultimo Atto*), also titled *The Last Four Days*, as the Italian dictator. Neither film made any impact among English-speaking audiences. He later reprised his Mussolini in the Libyan movie *Lion of the Desert*, starring opposite Anthony Quinn. The film was to sit on the shelf for a couple of years before it was released. It should not have been.

He was to give a Hemingway-like performance as a he-man author who returns from eight years spent in the Amazon jungle to discover that the world and his wife have changed. *Happy Birthday, Wanda Jane*, written by Kurt Vonnegut from his off-Broadway play, was a stylized comedy that failed to work on the screen. Even on the stage it had received negative reviews, Stanley Kauffmann describing it as 'full of callow wit, rheumatic invention and dormitory profundity'.

Director Mark Robson, with a low budget of $1.5m, worked quickly, shooting the film in twenty-seven days, but that tight schedule followed three weeks devoted to rehearsals on the set with the cast in costume so that not only could characterizations be fleshed out, but lighting and camera angles could be decided in advance. At least, it was not as bad as the lacklustre *Lolly Madonna XXX*, also called *The Lolly-Madonna War*, about a feud between two hillbilly families over a meadow, with Steiger and Robert Ryan as two warring patriarchs.

He also went to Rome, which during this period almost became a second home, to make a spaghetti Western, *Giù la Testa* (variously translated in English-speaking countries as *Duck, You Sucker!* and *A Fistful of Dynamite*). Made by Italy's foremost director of the genre, Sergio Leone, and with a pounding score by Ennio Morricone, it was not up to the standard of earlier collaborations, such as *A Fistful of Dollars* and *The Good, the Bad and the Ugly*, which had made Clint Eastwood into a star, or Leone's previous movie, his masterpiece *Once Upon a Time in the West*.

Giù la Testa teamed Rod, as a Mexican bandit, with James Coburn as a revolutionary Irish explosives expert, and concentrated on action, particularly in the version released outside Italy. Leone's edition for his local audience lasted twenty minutes longer and gave the actors an opportunity to develop their characters.

For director Francesco Rosi, Rod played doomed gangster Gene Giannini in the documentary-style *Lucky Luciano* (*A Proposito Luciano*), which starred Gian Maria Volonté as the Mafia boss who has lost his power but still keeps his position. Rosi's interest was less in Luciano himself than the way he was used by the FBI, the Mafia and Italian agencies for their own purposes and how complex relationships can be between the law and crime. For those expecting a thriller, it was a disappointment and even on a political level, it was flawed. Much of the dialogue was taken verbatim from official reports and interrogations and, in

135

the words of *Sight and Sound* critic Philip Strick, was 'literally unspeakable'. The film was cut by twenty-one minutes for its English-language release, which came eighteen months after it had opened in Italy. Rod's role was, Strick added, 'too small for him'.

He also made *The Heroes* (*Gli Eroi*), a dull caper movie set in the Second World War directed by Duccio Tessari with a cast of mixed nationalities that included Rod Taylor, Claude Brasseur and Terry-Thomas. Steiger played a good German officer who destroys an Allied convoy in the North African desert and discovers that it includes an ambulance containing two million pounds in secret funds. But the money is stolen and he sets out after it, as do a motley group of Allied soldiers. He has one of the few good lines in the film: 'There goes the new Germany,' he says, as his commanding officer's parachute fails to open, but there are few other compensations.

He fared little better in France, appearing in Claude Chabrol's tricksy thriller *Dirty Hands* (*Les Innocents aux Mains Sales*). Steiger had admired the director for his work but was disappointed in the direction he imposed on him, which was, in fact, little direction at all.

Steiger complained that Chabrol – always called by his surname – would direct via a TV monitor, rarely getting into the heat of the performing action. This also gave Chabrol room and opportunity to play chess, which was a constant diversion of his attention. Consequently, Steiger gave one of his most florid performances, putting on his moodiest faces. I told him this but he didn't blame Chabrol for the way it had gone. 'All right, so it didn't work,' he said.

In Germany, he made a war film, *Breakthrough*, or *Sergeant Steiner* (*Steiner – das eiserne Kreuz II*), which teamed him with Richard Burton and Robert Mitchum. All three actors were going through a period of appearing in bad films and this was not destined to change anything. Burton agreed to star because he was well paid and had become friends with its director, Andrew

McLaglen, when they worked on *The Wild Geese* a year or two earlier. What excuses the rest of the cast had, they kept to themselves. No doubt the money helped, but it was another flop.

In 1975 Rod went to Britain to make *Hennessy*, a thriller in which he played an Irish bomber who tries to blow up the Houses of Parliament and kill the Queen. It was the first feature for more than twenty years to try to come to terms with the Irish question, though it was followed four years later by a superior thriller, *The Long Good Friday*.

The audience's sympathy is centred on Steiger as Hennessy, whose wife and child are killed by British troops in Belfast; despite this, the movie eschews politics for the simpler pleasures of a revenge thriller. Nevertheless, British distributors viewed it with disfavour, mainly because it included newsreel of the Queen leaving Buckingham Palace for the State opening of Parliament, intercut with scenes of Rod bluffing his way into the building.

'It was so cleverly done it really looks as though the Queen is acting,' a spokesman for the British Board of Film Classification told the newspapers. Buckingham Palace first asked for the scenes with the Queen to be cut and then issued a statement together with the production company, AIP, which read:

> Before the film was made the company asked Buckingham Palace for permission to use parts of the relevant news film, and that permission was granted. It is now accepted, however, that when that permission was given there was, through no fault of the company, a misunderstanding on the part of the Palace as to the way in which the news film was to be used. The Palace has none the less confirmed its consent in this instance.

The film opened with a note that the shots of the Queen were not intended for use in a fictional context, and the Palace made it clear that they would turn down similar requests in future.

However, two major British distributors, EMI and Rank, both refused to show it in their cinemas and the film is rarely seen on television, though it was given a brief video release.

Steiger sold his costly apartment in New York in a move to cut down on his expenses, so that he would have a little more artistic freedom, which meant the luxury of turning down roles he did not want to play. 'To win your battle in this society you've got to have your cave, some food, and some kind of mate. Everything else is a luxury. The less you own, the less the danger of working for wall-to-wall carpeting,' he said, buying a smaller apartment in Greenwich Village.

He considered moving to London, because he liked the city and the English respect for acting. In the US, he found, you were always judged on your last performance, not on your whole body of work. He thought again of directing a screenplay he had written, though he knew many would assume that it was to do with his private life. Close friends had told him not to make it, but the opportunity was not to arise, anyway.

It was not difficult to turn down parts. The scripts he was being sent were poor. He was determined that he would not cheat his audience, that he would at least give them their money's worth, even if the film itself was less than good.

'There's no such thing as success,' he reflected. 'If you make it when you're young, you fight to sustain it for the rest of your life. You always fear that you're going to be replaced by younger talent, which is inevitable. What is important is making the effort, so at least you tried.'

His research into the life of Napoleon, who died comparatively young in his early fifties, seemed to concentrate his own mind. He wrote in his journal: 'I should hate, old, grey and gnarled, to look at a crack ever increasing in the ceiling above my beaten bed, to whisper to myself as I cried, I wish I had . . .'

His greatest disappointment was still to come. Rod had long wanted to make a film of the life of W. C. Fields and the chance arrived in 1976 with *W. C. Fields and Me*, based on the comedian's relationship with his mistress Carlotta Monti. Rod read all the books he could find on Fields and watched all his films. He came to the conclusion that *The Bank Dick* was the quintessence of the man, and that Fields' drawling manner of speech was deliberately exaggerated for the screen.

But the experience was not a happy one. He clashed with Valerie Perrine, who played Carlotta and commented, 'I don't know how someone playing W. C. Fields could be so totally without humour.' Yet later Rod wept in a television interview telling how Carlotta herself had watched him play the role and hugged him afterwards, calling him by Fields' nickname, 'Woody'. 'There were people in the cast more interested in publicity than acting,' he says. And, also, it has to be said, in various chemical substances which helped give them a kick-start into the dramatics.

Indeed, Steiger has confessed that he doesn't think he is a natural comedian, if by that you feel it is spraying off sweetness and light like a garden sprinkler. But comedians themselves are seldom as funny off-stage as on, especially somebody as complicated as Fields himself. Where I think Steiger succeeded is in establishing the nature of a man who had been reared in the clammy origins of old-time vaudeville. He had the integrity of that time.

A friend of mine did a sketch on radio, which an ageing Fields liked; he rang to ask if he could use it. Honoured, my friend said of course; that wasn't enough for Fields: he sent my friend ten dollars, so that the sketch became his. Because that's what you did when he was a young man in music-hall: you paid for your schtick.

Personally, I thought that the British comedian Les Dawson was a better Fields than Steiger. But nobody in Hollywood would ever have given Dawson that kind of chance.

So the film was not well received. Critic Les Keyser wrote, 'Just the sort of memorial Fields might have wished for Baby

Leroy.' Judith Crist condemned it as 'a stupid and pointless slander,' and the British magazine *Sight and Sound* commented, 'Steiger's impersonation largely keeps pace with the overriding vulgarity of the enterprise.'

But worse was to come. While Rod was playing tennis with a friend, Caroll Rosenbloom, owner of the Los Angeles Rams football team, he felt a sudden pain in his chest and collapsed on court. He was rushed to hospital and, at Rosenbloom's insistence, given tests that revealed that vessels in his heart were severely blocked. He was given a heart bypass operation as quickly as possible. The event shocked him severely.

It also put his career in trouble. Producers are chary of employing actors who may drop dead at any moment and thus jeopardize a film. Insurance companies often refuse to insure such actors or demand impossibly high premiums. Rod was forced to take whatever parts came his way. The director John Huston had the same problem at about the same time. He took on a couple of Canadian movies just to prove to the actuaries that he could make a movie and survive.

Steiger said: 'I did a lot of films – some of which you'd call garbage – just to prove to the insurance companies that I wouldn't drop dead in front of the cameras. I took any job as long as it wasn't too disgraceful. I always say I'm sixty per cent virgin and forty per cent whore. As long as you can keep away from fifty-fifty, you're still safe.'

A low-budget movie, variously titled *Jim Buck* and *Portrait of a Hitman*, re-united him with Jack Palance for the first time since *The Big Knife*. It was a dull and tedious work, in which Rod played, yet again, a gangster. He hires Palance's killer to shoot a surgeon, unaware that the man had once saved the hitman's life. Rod brought a repertoire of tricks to the role: sudden glares, smouldering anger, shouts of fury and a threatening *bonhomie* in his quieter moments, but the part was poorly written, and consisted of little but reactions to the actions of others. There was not much he could do to give it any credibility, and nothing he could have done would have saved the film – it was beyond rescue.

In Canada, he made *Wolf Lake*, a lacklustre movie, which gave him another hectoring role as a man who lost his son in Vietnam and is confronted with a deserter in Canada. It was so bad that its release was delayed for two years. Then there was the whimsical and forgettable *The Lucky Star*, about a young boy's fantasy life of cowboys that helped him to survive his wartime experiences in Holland in 1940. Steiger played a Nazi officer. This was followed by *Klondyke Fever*, directed by Peter Carter and based on a Jack London story, in which he played Soapy Smith.

The films he made in America were little better: *F.I.S.T.* teamed him with Sylvester Stallone and Peter Boyle in Norman Jewison's film of a corrupt union boss, based on the life of Jimmy Hoffa. Interestingly, though, Steiger emerged from that with a fondness for Stallone which seemed very much at odds with Stallone's brutalized reputation for movies such as *Rocky* and *Rambo*. 'I found him a real gentleman and his acting was not the kind of short-cut technique I might have believed if I had only judged the movies I had seen him in.'

The Amityville Horror, released in 1979, was taken from a bestselling book about a haunted house that claimed to be based on fact. Directed by Stuart Rosenberg, the only distinguished thing about it was the score written by Lalo Schifrin, which was nominated for an Oscar. Rod did, as Pauline Kael put it, 'his padre number'. She added, 'His spiritual agony was enough to shatter the camera lens.' *Love and Bullets* was a mundane thriller directed by Stuart Rosenberg and starring Charles Bronson as an FBI agent chasing gangster's moll Jill Ireland. Rod, in knee-jerk casting, played a Mafia boss and, perhaps out of boredom, as he was asked to flesh out a character that was hardly written, resorted to an over-the-top performance. The film flopped, and was hardly released before ending up on video.

'I did everything I was offered,' he says. 'I had no idea how the film would turn out, I only wanted to show everyone I was still capable of hard work.'

Rod, recalled Claire Bloom recently, always put acting first. He regarded it with a seriousness she could never match or even begin to appreciate. 'I couldn't understand how anyone could take himself so seriously,' she has said. She observed that he was most sure of his own existence when he was playing someone else. He really believed in the roles he played, becoming that person. I detect a similarity to Peter Sellers, who once told me that he saw himself in the mirror while he was kissing a girl. 'That person in the looking glass seemed more real than I was.'

But in the 1980s, that absorption in the life of another became very difficult to maintain. It was one thing to become the crooked lawyer Charlie or Marty or redneck police chief Gillespie. Those roles were well-written. They provided scope and scale. They were characters he could drape around himself like a second skin.

His boredom grew into a serious depression. He was unhappy when he wasn't acting, and unhappier when he was. 'Acting wasn't doing anything for me at all,' he said, which was hardly surprising considering the parts he was being offered. It was not the first time he had felt in the doldrums. After he had won the Oscar for *In the Heat of the Night* in 1967, no one had offered him a role for nearly a year.

That had had a devastating effect on him. He withdrew into himself, not talking to Claire or Anna, spending hours lying on a sofa watching sport on television – American football was his favourite. Claire found his state near-catatonic. He was finally roused by the offer of the leading role in *The Sergeant*, playing an army officer who becomes obsessed by a handsome private.

But now he knew that such roles would not often come his way. He tried to combat his depression with female company.

142

There was a brief dalliance with a psychiatrist, Dr Dana Longino. 'She's got me thinking about marriage again,' he told journalists, but he was still in bad shape. His second heart bypass operation in 1980 had made producers chary of employing him.

Discussing his experience of working with James Mason with Mason's biographer Sheridan Morley, Rod could have been talking about himself in these black days of middle age. It was as if then, in 1958, he had been granted an insight into what lay ahead for himself:

There was something oddly tragic about Mr Mason. You felt that things in this life were eating away at him, and that he was always in a tremendous kind of emotional pain which he was bravely trying to hide. So the façade was always there, and he seemed to take pride in putting up a front as though everything was all right, when you knew that deep down it couldn't possibly be.

He was a great technician and it may have been that, like me, he got too far away from the theatre where we both spent the first decade of our careers, and then could never get back in touch with it. But there was something churning inside of him, and although he never let it show in his work, you could always sense it. He was a tenacious son of a bitch, and a great survivor, but I think he was maybe too intelligent for some of the work he had to do in movies.

Rod's depression lasted several years. 'You begin to lose self-esteem,' he says. 'You don't walk, you don't shave and if no one was watching you'd go to the bathroom right where you were sitting.' He'd lie in bed thinking, You'll never act again. Why bother? You're no good. The same few thoughts going round and round in his head.

Rod had once remarked, 'If the part excites me, I'll play it anywhere – in films, television, radio, or on the stage – because I'm an actor. That's my job, that's what I am supposed to do.'

He had always taken pride in himself as an actor. 'Acting is my bullfighting,' he said.

Unfortunately, he was being forced into the arena with half-grown bulls. But that had its compensations. A man had to provide for himself and his family. 'You've got to bring food into the house before you can start talking about ideals,' he said.

By now, his home on the Pacific Ocean at Malibu was paid for. He had managed to hold on to it through his divorces and it housed his most treasured possessions.

'I have tried to maintain my self-respect in a house with good food, and still hold on to the luxury of my naïve ideals,' he said. 'You can become so tired of fighting for what you believe that you lose sight of what you are doing.'

The split with Claire Bloom had contributed in an accumulating way to that depression; so had the divorce from Sherry.

It was only when he met Paula Ellis, a woman young enough to be his daughter, that life began to take on some meaning again, and recovery was slow. He would lie in bed all day or get up and stare out at the Pacific Ocean, hardly saying a word. With Paula's help he sought medical advice, discovering that his condition was a clinical one and that he could take drugs to provide him with the balance he needed to get through the days.

They were married in 1986. My wife Pat and I went to his wedding reception – after a brief register office wedding – at Crockfords, the sporting club in Curzon Street, whose owner let Rod have a champagne-fuelled party. It was, indeed, a glitzy do, with Rod beckoning Pat and me to his side, a position we rarely left during the evening. It was as though we were the only people he wanted to talk to. Afterwards, we learned that he had been on anti-depressant pills, so we could take that as a compliment – or not. What was apparent, though, was the love Paula and Steiger felt for each other. She was the hostess, but whenever he looked up towards her, she was there. He acted as though she might be spirited away at any moment. That dreadful vanishing act was to happen years later . . .

Pat instinctively recognized that Paula, despite her youth, was the best thing that could have happened to Steiger. After some months Paula rang us and said: 'Just to let you know that Rod's all right. There've been some rumours around that he'd died or retired or just disappeared. He's back on form. We thought you'd like to know.'

Steiger was told that alcohol, of which he and I were fond, was chemically alien to his constitution. Once when Pat and I sat waiting for him in the foyer of the Savoy Hotel, Rod and Paula arrived around ten minutes late. 'Sorry for that,' boomed Steiger, 'we had to go to the AA.' I pondered that news. 'I didn't know you had a car over here that needed the Automobile Association.' Then we all looked at each other, burst out laughing, and realized that the AA referred to was Alcoholics Anonymous. Not that Steiger was addicted: it was just that it helped to get encouragement. But the depression continued.

At one point, it got so bad that he loaded a shotgun. He thought he might have to do away with himself. But sanity prevailed. He gave the gun to a friend. 'I couldn't, so I then locked myself in a basement room for three days. I didn't sleep. I clawed my flesh, scratched my eyes, totally demeaned myself. Paula was the one who took care of me. She never accused me or gave me a sense of stigma about my illness.

'That is the true definition of love. Without Paula I might not have made it.'

9

S teiger rang me with joy in his voice and delight in his heart. With his son beside him, he had just unveiled his star on Hollywood's Walk of Fame, a boulevard which had once seemed unattainable to him in a community where glamour was the equivalent of success; a certain kind of glamour that is. If you had a metaphorical gleam on your pants for reasons of poverty or failure then that didn't count. 'I never thought I'd make it,' said Rod. 'It was hell down there.' He was referring to what Oscar Wilde called *De Profundis*; that he managed to rise from those awful depths of depression owes as much to Paula's care and tending as to his inherent strength.

Having now come through the bleak years of depression Steiger can distance himself from it to give lectures on the subject, to those who have been told by their relatives and friends 'to snap out of it'. He knows that depression is something more profound than that, and how few doctors will treat it as the chemical imbalance which it can so often be – and is, in his case. As well as lecturing he frequently attends charity functions to support the idea that mental illness is not something to be ashamed of, but to be aware of. At one of these charity dinners General Schwarzkopf, who had been in charge of the Desert Storm series of battles against Iraq, asked for him to be sat next to him.

Steiger was flattered, but thought he might get something out of the encounter. So he asked the General how he felt about sending young men out to die or, even worse, to be mutilated.

Good after-dinner conversation. 'It was interesting to see how human the man was. He had been profoundly depressed by the experience. His imagination was overwrought with the thought of the deaths that were to happen.'

Steiger himself can joke about his own depressions with a kind of black humour. 'After I'd had my first heart by-pass operation the doctors told me that the anaesthetic might have depressive side-effects afterwards. The wrong thing to say!

'You know you should never say that sort of thing to an actor, especially one like me, because I took it to heart. 'Cos I'm going to have the biggest blues ever. Just to prove them right. Only I've enlarged the script to fit my personality.'

As a scientific thesis it hardly works, but as a humorous punchline it's as effective as any other. And, at least, Steiger makes it seem plausible.

Steiger can help others because he has been there, done that. He has climbed that steep hill of neurosis which so often becomes psychosis.

But he suffered humiliations at that time – the memory of which he still carries with him. As he came out of the depression he was only too well aware of the need to earn a buck, to feed his family. And he was asked to audition for the role of one of the elder Irishmen for the film *Far and Away*, starring Tom Cruise and his wife, Nicole Kidman. It seemed a heaven-sent opportunity.

Ron Howard was the director. Now Howard is the kind of director you may have heard of, but you can't remember the titles of any movies he has made. Steiger felt himself to be brought low at having to 'read' the role, anyway. Didn't Howard have any trust in what had been done in the past? Not so, it seems.

He also insisted that Steiger wear a wig. And he wanted the audition to be on video tape. 'I hated that. Because those tapes usually form part of the after-dinner entertainment on the Bel-Air circuit, so that guests can see stars making fools of themselves. But what could I do? I needed the work. I desperately needed the work. But Howard – the cocksucker – insisted that I be video-taped.'

Steiger got turned down for the role. 'I'll never forgive Ron Howard for that humiliation. It showed he had no respect for me or my work. He was just using me. I hope I gave him some fun for his dinner parties. I know, sure as God, I didn't have any – fun, that is.'

I expressed sympathy, but Steiger had hauled himself erect again. 'That's Hollywood for you. That's what it's like to be kicked when you're down. And I'm glad that *Far and Away* was such a rotten movie: it fitted its director.'

It needed more than drugs to energize Rod from his somnolent dislike of himself and life. In 1980, he was given a better role than he had enjoyed in a decade in *Cattle Annie and Little Britches*, but it was a western made at a time when the appetite for such films was on the wane. Indeed, the film sat on the shelf for a year before it was released, since two other westerns had failed at the box office. It was given no more than a week at a New York cinema before being replaced by *Outland*, which, ironically, was *High Noon* set in outer space.

Cattle Annie and Little Britches, at least, was original in its approach, following the adventures of two adolescent girls who, their heads full of romanticized pulp fiction, join a bunch of outlaws headed by the ageing Bill Doolin, played by Burt Lancaster with weary authority.

Rod had the role of a determined US marshal chasing the Doolin gang. The director Lamont Johnson, himself an actor, concentrated on controlling the performances of an excellent cast that included Amanda Plummer and Diane Lane as the girls. Pauline Kael wrote of Rod's acting that he was 'probably more contained than he has been in years'.

Diane Lane told me that to work with Steiger was 'an enormous privilege. He is, after all, a legend and you listen to everything he has to say about acting. Not that he said much. He seemed a bit tired, would slump in his chair and look exhausted. When he was available for conversation, he sparkled. He really did.'

Maybe Diane Lane was just being polite (she's one of the few stars I've interviewed who wrote to thank me for the privilege!), but she seemed genuine and, really, rather in awe.

Steiger had another chance to shine in *The Chosen*, directed by Jeremy Paul Kagan, and based on the bestseller by Chaim Potok exploring the tense relationship between a father and son. Originally, Maximilian Schell was cast as the father, a staunchly orthodox rabbi, with Rod playing a family friend. But Rod persuaded Schell to switch roles, excited by the challenge of the last scene, in which the rabbi explains to his son (Robby Benson) that he seemed cold and uncaring and out of love. *Variety*'s critic wrote, 'Steiger gives an exceptional performance as the somewhat tyrannical but loving patriarch.' The film, for all its quality, failed to find favour with audiences.

I know it is one of Steiger's favourite films and his religious dance towards the end was an overspilling of divine devotion that audiences long remember – not just because of its audacity in going so far over the top, but because of the obvious sincerity that fuels the whole situation.

'But how are you going to keep 'em down on the farm, after they've seen Paree?' It was still downhill most of the way in the films that followed. He went to Yugoslavia to play a resistance leader in *That Summer of White Roses*, directed by Rajko Grlic, and also starring Tom Conti and Susan George, who was producing the film with her husband Simon McCorkindale. Rod liked the role because it was a chance to work in Europe, and the opportunity to play a good person rarely came his way. He saw his character as an angel, someone sent down from above to do good in the world, though he knew his director would be unhappy with his interpretation. However much he was attracted to the character, the completed film was a vapid, over-sentimentalized affair that barely got a release. However, it did give Steiger a chance to make a good friend out of Tom Conti, taking my wife and me along to his north London home to meet him.

Then he went to Germany to make *The Magic Mountain* (*Der Zauberberg*), based on Thomas Mann's novel. Directed by Hans W. Geissendoerfer, it cast him opposite Marie-France Pisier and Charles Aznavour. Rod has never seen the finished film, which was hardly glimpsed outside Germany.

But Rod was still being offered, and taking, roles he might have wished to avoid, where his name could add a little class to run-of-the-mill material. He made *The Naked Face*, which was directed and written by Bryan Forbes from a Sidney Sheldon novel. Rod and Elliott Gould played cops who suspect psychiatrist Roger Moore of murdering one of his patients.

But most of the roles he was offered were much worse. *The Kindred* was a mix of horror and science fiction, in which teenagers are menaced by a sea-monster cloned from the genes of one of them. The *Daily Mail* critic wrote, 'The only way of getting full value from its tired and tatty thrills is to send someone you dislike to see it,' adding that Rod, 'treated to massive close-ups, reminding one of an Arran Pilot potato in a toupee, wanders through as a mad scientist dabbling in genetic engineering and grave robbery.'

Catch the Heat, also known as *Feel the Heat*, cast him as a South American drug baron. In 1988 he appeared in a TV Western: *Desperado; Avalanche at Devil's Ridge*, in which he played a rancher whose daughter is kidnapped. In another TV film, *Passion and Paradise*, about a real-life unsolved murder, he played the victim, the millionaire Sir Harry Oakes. Then he went down the social scale to rant as the murderous head of a family of killers in the dire horror movie *American Gothic*.

He began to sound disillusioned, even though his depression was behind him. 'I should have done better films,' he says. 'I should have done more stage. You become a commodity in this business after a while. People expect certain things of a Rod

150

Steiger part in the way they expect certain things of a brand of washing powder.'

Casting directors still saw him in strong, often unpleasant roles. Rod was well aware of the type of characters he was usually asked to play: 'There's a certain amount of strength in them, a certain amount of isolation. Loneliness. Anger. Power.'

A better role was offered him by Yorkshire TV, who were planning to make a three-part series of Gerald Seymour's thriller *The Glory Boys*, about an Israeli scientist targeted by Palestinian terrorists while visiting London. Rod eagerly accepted the role, and found himself playing opposite Anthony Perkins, another American actor who had known better times and who had been miscast as a London security agent hired to protect Rod.

There was tension on the set between them, not helped by the fact that Rod had insisted on a large trailer, so that there was room for Paula. He was given the biggest available. Perkins' was much smaller, and he resented it. Rod was also unhappy at Perkins' habit of swallowing amphetamine just before a take, to give him that air of nervous tension familiar from many of his performances. 'He was so jittery and jinxed by the chemicals he was taking that it was possible to feel sorry for him. But not often. I thought he was putting the film in jeopardy,' Steiger complained.

Perkins argued that Rod was stealing the scenes from him, and speaking just before Perkins had finished saying his lines. Director Mike Ferguson found that both his stars were on edge, with Rod becoming aggressive and Perkins withdrawn. Rod rewrote some of his lines and would ask for a close-up when he thought his acting required it. Despite his recent heart operation, Rod gave an excellent performance within the confines of the role, which, ironically perhaps, ends with him dying of a heart attack on a flight home to Israel. Steiger did not see it as a bad omen.

The real recovery began in 1988 when he found himself among an excellent, co-operating cast in Pat O'Connor's *The*

January Man. A thriller about a disgraced cop who tracks down a serial killer, it starred Kevin Kline, Susan Sarandon, Harvey Keitel, Danny Aiello and Alan Rickman. But Rod's performance as a domineering mayor of New York City is way over the top, as he himself admits.

It was one of the first roles in which he experienced pleasure in acting again after his paralysing depression. 'That day I began to feel some of my power come back, some of the feelings I was used to,' he says. 'And what I did was not so much to play the scene as celebrate the fact that I could feel again as a human being. And then I went crazy to see how far I could go.' Unfortunately, no one was prepared to restrain him. And there are times when, as he sees it, he does need somebody to hold him back. Somebody he can respect and respond to.

10

Film critics live in shadowland, a world of artifice and dreams. As do, with more immediacy, actors. So it is, blundering through mirages, that we sometimes, just occasionally, make a contact that becomes an embrace, in the way that it happened to myself and Steiger.

Steiger, though – such is the nature imposed upon him by his temperament and the power of his calling – has also rubbed egos with some of the most beautiful and provocative women in the world. Not that he likes talking about these intimacies – his wife, Paula, after all, was his once and future queen. Even now, when he talks about her his eyes brim with tears, as they so often do when he thinks about something near and dear to him. I take good vibes from that, because a friend of mine interviewed Steiger for BBC radio and said that, talking about me, Steiger leaked tears. He wears his heart on his sleeve and – in his roles – the art follows in due course. It is that passion which has fuelled him for his greatest performances – and his worst.

I put it to him that this memoir of our friendship should have a feminine dimension, an acknowledgement of all the women he has loved in his life before – and after – Paula. After all, a man who has been married four times – thus legitimizing at least four affairs – must, by the nature of things, have had other relationships not so blessed with rectitude.

All he wanted, he said, was a tribute to the women who have – and I quote – 'educated me by their love and to whom I give thanks for their kindness and entertainment'. He really does like women, you see.

The libido list goes back to school days and a girl called Jane Scanlon he knew when he was six years old. 'It's that old cliché about my carrying her satchel to school. But that's exactly what I did. Oh, and we sometimes held hands.'

Later there were other schoolgirls such as Helen and Nancy. And as a Naval torpedo man there were one-night stands, which – because of curtailed leave – were more often three-hour stopovers.

He remembers Victoria, 'a charming black lady', and a girl called Julie, whom he first met in Cairo and, later, in Paris.

There was Sally Gracie of course, his first wife, and then Claire Bloom – the Hutchinsons' first encounter with his amours. Then Sherry Nelson, now sadly dead, whose spirited liveliness endeared her to Steiger and us. She may have extracted alimony from him, but he remembers her personality with some affection.

There were the actresses Irene Papas, Joan Crawford and, later, Vanessa Redgrave and Diana Dors, who has already been mentioned. Well, of course, they made a very bad film together in Hollywood, *The Unholy Wife*, and Steiger still insists that this wild child of her time, this rebellious starlet of the British Rank Organziation, 'was one of the frankest, most honest women I ever met. The trouble was her husband, Denis Hamilton . . .'

Amplifying his memory of that early run-in with Hamilton, he says that Hamilton – who broadcast an overt gangsterism with a hype I know he perceived as a glamour to correspond to his wife's – barged into Steiger's dressing-room, shouting and bawling about adultery.

'I knew he carried a gun because he had shown it to me, as though showing off a penis – mine's bigger than yours! – so I sat quiet while he raved on. Then he started yelling about "stupid actors" and that really riled me. It was the word "stupid" that got to me. So I forgot about the possible gun and grabbed

154

him and pushed him out into the corridor. Amazingly, he went quietly.'

Distanced from his brutal screen image, he regards women as ladies (he still sees his alcoholic mother that way): he puts women on a pedestal, not to look up their skirts but to revere their gentle difference. I once said he ought to have been a Roman Catholic with a bent towards Mariolatry, but he said he couldn't stand the incense though he loved the ceremony.

But even in the rough-trade image he portrays in movies there is always a charm in the way he treats ladies, even if he kills them: tender is the might.

The acclaimed New Zealand actress, Kerry Fox, made *The Last Tattoo* with him for director John Reid. She told critic Marianne Gray:

> I really enjoyed working with Rod, but he was in an unfortunate position working with John Reid because John didn't know how to direct him and didn't. Rod remembered every line and his work was so very full of passion. He believed in giving everything . . . unfortunately, John Reid never told him when to give.
>
> Rod was very kind to me, enormously generous. I remember in one scene, the ballroom scene, when we were having difficulties about how to do it, he whispered to me: 'Just fly with it, just fly, fly!' I think he is missing a layer of skin – he is definitely not in the slightest thick-skinned. He and Paula were great together. She's pretty hot, you know. They were a great couple.

I think women sense the surging passion below the surface of the Steiger charm, the maelstrom that churned itself in the illness that was clinical depression. There is one woman, though, whose legend he considers inviolate: Marlene Dietrich. He was doing a TV play live with her daughter, Maria, and technicalities came between him and his acting. A gunshot had to be ignited

155

off-stage. It didn't happen and he was not cued that it had not gone off.

Then it didn't go off again, so that he was not aware that he was supposed to have been shot. So frustrated was he that he reeled back, tears flowing down his cheeks, and fell against a piece of scenery. It stunned him. When he came round the show was over and above him, solidifying in the darkness, was the famous face with a cigarette holder in the mouth.

'Are you all right?' asked Marlene Dietrich. 'You were magnificent, you know! Quite magnificent!'

Rod Steiger has never forgotten that: 'She gave me cookies she had made herself. I know she was supposed to have been unkind to her daughter, and I wonder how much her late-blooming kindness to others was guilt.' And remembering it, he weeps a little at how lovely she was. And how kind. And, as he puts it, how ladylike.

When Rod Steiger acts, he is ripping out emotions from himself. It is a risky business: a man can get hurt that way. That's why he suffered nervous depressions.

His profession becomes a disturbing dichotomy between what is seen on screen and what is known in life. Steiger's roles may allow weakness to be glimpsed through the authority of the performance – as in Charlie in *On the Waterfront* – but only via the priest in *The Amityville Horror* does mania take over. Rod Steiger has always, in real life, put on a brave front.

But just as he will rush full-tilt at a part, so he took on his depressions as though they formed a fearful adversary that had to be beaten. Knowing that clinical depression was his enemy he read all he could about it and now participates in every occasion that tries to make 'normals' understand what bigoted tradition has tried to make extraordinary. At the behest of the National Mental Health Authority he will give lectures on the subject, using himself as his own prime example. Other actors, like Jason Robards and Patty Duke – who may not have had

Rod's personal angst – are part of that awareness drive. The mail he gets shows that he is very much not alone and that his experiences are helpful and healthful to those who have not the gift of celebrity. He takes pills in the morning and at night and these anti-depressants seem to work in lifting his spirits.

He was mainly helped, of course, by his wife Paula, who presented him with a baby boy, Michael Winston, born on 8 February 1993. In 1992, when I was organizing a celebration of his work for the National Film Theatre, he had rung me to announce that Paula was pregnant. He was boastful, as so many Americans are where their potency is at stake. 'Sixty-seven!' he told me, and himself, unbelievingly; trying to convince both of us. 'Not bad for a guy of sixty-seven. It's a good omen for the National Film Theatre, isn't it? That's what Paula says and I tend to agree.'

In those days he agreed a lot with Paula.

As I wrote for the NFT booklet, 'Whether wringing an emotion stone-dry or playing it sopping wet, the plunge into character is always exhilarating. When he goes over the top he takes us with him in terms of sympathy; like the director Robert Altman, he is falling from a cliff: no way back; in terms of drama he takes no prisoners.'

At well over seventy, Rod Steiger is an acting role-model whose time has come again. The School of Steiger is a class surreptitiously attended by some of the most enthusiastically belligerent of male actors. David Benzali, the bone-domed attorney of the first series of television's *Murder One*, was once at a reception with Steiger and told him, 'You are my hero, my favourite actor!'

Steiger's smile was like ice breaking. 'So I should be. You've been living off my style for a long time. You even look like me – though I don't suppose you can help that.'

Steiger chuckles affectionately: 'Of course I sweetened it all with a laugh, but I meant what I said. And I said the same thing

157

to Robert De Niro when he did such a carbon copy of my Al Capone in his film of *The Untouchables*.

'I suppose it's all some sort of compliment. But Marlon Brando and I created our characters from scratch, from the ground up. We tried not to go to other actors for our ideas. I think that, at least, we attempted originality.'

I last saw Rod in London when he came over for a small role as the father to Jason Patrick in *Incognito*. Patrick plays a master art forger, and if you can believe that you can believe anything. The title, though, has a cruel relevance to Rod who dropped out of sight for all those years with clinical depression. He's more eloquent about those suicidal lows now: 'It's like being up to your neck in frozen excrement,' he says, remembering his manager Jess Morgan's chill warning: 'You're going to have to do something, because people are forgetting who or where you are.' It is a fearful threat to any actor, that you may fade from recollection. After all, actors are people who are trying to create memorials while they are still alive. Perhaps that's when Steiger started to overcome the overwhelming.

He found himself coming out of it when he heard Paula screaming at one of his specialists: 'Will you forget who he is and treat him as a patient?' For there is, as Paula recognized, a way in which a patient's celebrity rubs off on the doctor who is treating him or her. Certainly, it happens in Hollywood where fame is the coin by which reputations are exchanged and established.

Now he displaces as much space and energy as ever he did; his passions are charged and various. My wife, Pat, once asked him why he went to hear his daughter Anna perform, when he said he disliked modern opera so much.

'Not that I like what she sings, though I know she does it splendidly, but I sit and watch and listen and I think, That's my baby up there! *Oklahoma!* it's not. But she's my baby! And that makes up for so much.'

158

Now, he is at once acerbic and vulnerable. When we had luncheon at a fashionably swish hotel where he was staying he said, 'the fourth course should have been a stomach pump'. Vulnerable? His friend, special-effects maestro, Stan Winston, after whom Steiger's son, Michael Winston, is named, wound him up for his interview with the director Tim Burton for a part in *Mars Attacks!*, a wonderfully bizarre science-fiction idea based on trade cards which were handed out in the thirties.

Stan built up our first interview by telling me that Burton dressed all in black and was very introverted. He said I was not to intimidate him, which is the reputation Stan thinks I have.

So I went to Tim Burton's office, all apprehensive and worried – yes, I did, Tom, there's no need to look so incredulous – and he uncoiled from his chair and shouted 'Maestro!' So there we were bawling Italian at each other for the next few hours, as though we had known each other for years.

Rod Steiger makes friends like that – and, I suppose, enemies. He expects the best until he learns the worst. His role as a manic US commander in *Mars Attacks!* had to be delivered from behind sunglasses, a difficult feat for any actor, but he is happiest about ad-libbing from a Winston Churchill speech to put across the man. But in the next breath he is attacking a film he'd just made for TV: 'It also starred Farrah Fawcett and it was written and produced by this schmuck who thought he was Arthur Miller, but wasn't.

'He tried to cut off my balls during the shoot, and I don't want to be vindictive – though I am – but I'm happy to say that ABC turned down his next project.'

It's my belief that Steiger bears grudges, like a haversack, but is too busy to unload them or do anything about them. He is too busy playing games with ideas and interpretations. His friend, Anthony Hopkins, had appeared in a sadly misguided story of

159

Picasso. 'Did I ever show you *my* Picasso?' he asked me. I say no.

'Well, here goes.'

He shifted his face as though it were soft wax, narrowed his eyes into a glare and, indeed, was Picasso. A pity he never played him.

While on the subject of vulnerability, Rod came to see us once wearing a toupee. He asked my wife if she liked it. 'No,' she said. 'You look so much better and more masculine without such a disguise.' He never wore a toupee when we were in his company after that.

He is also amazingly sensitive in ways you wouldn't believe; a sensitivity that comes from left field. Some years ago I had a heart problem. Rod rang to say I ought to go into hospital. Later Paula rang to suggest that Rod would pay for me to go to an American surgeon he knew. 'He didn't want to approach you direct,' she said, 'because we love you and know it might embarrass you.' I didn't take up the offer, but in this case it was me that wept.

Steiger rates friendship and kindness above all other qualities. That's why he won't hear a word against Frank Sinatra. Lee J. Cobb, who was the bullying union leader in *On the Waterfront*, was a great gambler. Sinatra, who had never met him, heard he was in hospital and indebted over his head. Sinatra paid off those debts, 'as a gift for some great acting'.

Great acting is what Rod Steiger has achieved through his career. If he has made mistakes at least they're honest mistakes. It is my theory that he makes eyeball contact with a role and stares it out, until it submits to his interpretation. He is a confrontational sort of guy. He has mellowed, though. 'I have to work sometimes in things I don't like just to pay my bills. My first obligation used to be to my work. Now it is to my health and my family. After that comes acting.'

One of his most impressive mistakes was Simon Callow's

An extraordinary performance. Steiger in
The Pawnbroker (1965) with Jaime Sanchez.

Small-town police chief
Steiger comes to terms
with black city cop
Sidney Poitier for *In the
Heat of the Night* (1967).
Years later a young
Hollywood whizzkid
asked an auditioning
Steiger if he could
'manage' a Southern
redneck accent.

As the redneck sheriff in *In the Heat of the Night*, Steiger not
only won an Oscar, but director Norman Jewison later said,
'It was one of the most moving performances I've ever seen.'

In *Waterloo* (1971), Rod Steiger proved his over-the-top ability to upstage the might of the Russian army (used as back-up in the battle scenes). As Napoleon, Steiger was always in command.

Steiger with his fourth wife Paula, baby Michael Winston and Oscar – Steiger's the one wearing the jewellery.

A new role for Steiger. The acting coach presents an
Oscar to his student, US president Bill Clinton.

(*Opposite*) Three amigos. Steiger with Jeff Goldblum and
John Goodman in a perfectly posed 'informal' moment.

A meeting of great minds…the author with Steiger
on the set of *Across the Bridge* (1957).

Steiger and the author, a few years later, at London's Langham
Hilton. Is Steiger adding more scurrilous anecdotes to
the book? No – he's probably writing another poem.

Steiger in his usual assertive mood as the nuke-'em-high
general in *Mars Attacks!* (1997), in which director Tim Burton
took on the aliens – and lost.

Steiger finally makes it as a 'Boulevard' star. The author notes it as one of the rare moments when Steiger has been on his knees.

Another great performance – Steiger charms his audience at the NFT (1992).

version of Carson McCullers' Southern Gothic *The Ballad of the Sad Café*, with an admiring Vanessa Redgrave. Steiger's role was as a slack-bellied, baggy-trousered preacher, an underwritten part of which he had had high expectations. It didn't work out that way. His contribution to high acting was to be knocked senseless.

But he had in it what he thought of as 'one of the most beautiful speeches I ever had to say in a motion picture':

I think that was why they wanted me to do that part. The speech is one of the essences of the film. It is a discourse on the nature of love. If you don't have somebody who can put that across you might be in a lot of trouble. Working on that kind of film is like a barometer for me. It sorts out the difference between the striving artist and the artist who is full of bullshit. You find out who really likes to act. It's the kind of movie we need a lot more of instead of car chases and Mafia stuff.

At the National Film Theatre celebration five years ago, he spotted Simon Callow, his one-time director for *Sad Café*, in the audience. 'Simon, hi! How about some more work, Simon? You've been ignoring me, Simon.' Callow is rarely lost for words; this time he didn't say anything but – I swear – he blushed.

Until *Mars Attacks!*, Steiger wasn't much acclaimed in his later movies. There was *Guilty As Charged*, a black comedy with Rod as a religious maniac with his own electric chair with which to execute criminals. Then came his small role as a washed-up actor in Robert Altman's satiric Hollywood comedy, *The Player*. 'I've never known an actor who can look so hang-dog to order as Rod,' Altman told me. 'He is truly one of the last of the greats.'

Other films came and went unnoticed: shits that pass in the night. *The Twilight Murders*, *The Dakota Murders*, slaughters that make for titles if not drama. In *The Specialist*, with Sylvester Stallone, he plays a Godfather as I've mentioned. He is supposed to show his contempt for Sharon Stone and wanted to spit in her face. Even aware of her looks, she insisted on his slapping her. Saliva, I suppose, would indicate real contempt, not make-believe violence.

He made one film in Europe and John Hurt, his co-star, greeted him with: 'This director is a case. It's all you can do to keep your temper.' Steiger kept his cool with a man who didn't know what he was doing, but insisted on telling everyone he did. 'He was a bastard. When I left he said "Lovely working with you, Rod. When I'm in America I'll come and see you". Timing is everything, Tom. I paused for a couple of minutes. Then I said: "I'll be out".'

That remembrance brought him to a melancholic soliloquy. 'I'm an old man in a business where they are targeting audiences of twenty-year-olds. America worships youth and has a fear of death. There aren't many good roles for the over-seventies.'

If there are, though, Rod Steiger has grabbed them. As with all of us, the stories of our life embellish our minds like *The Illustrated Man* or Woman. But there is a philosophy that evolves through these pictures, as I have tried to indicate in this book. Thirty or more years ago he put his personal feelings into a film script about an actor, *The Untold Story*. This has remained untold. He believes that if a man creates more beauty than he destroys you must classify him as good. If he destroys more beauty than he creates you must rate him as evil.

On that score, Rod Steiger remains not only a Hollywood survivor, still capable of surprising us, but someone who is on the side of the angels.

Or of the birds. The other week he rang me from Malibu with a story he thought I might like, about a farmer who complained that his hens weren't happy or laying good eggs. He was advised to get a super-rooster, who then went through the females as though he'd never had sex before. The hens cheered up and the eggs were great. Then the farmer noticed that the rooster was lying on his back, eyes closed tight, his claws wide open: dead.

Above him a vast vulture circled with the air of someone who knew a good meal was about due.

The farmer rushed over to the rooster. 'You can't be dead! You must be alive! You had such a great time with those hens! Say you're all right!'

The rooster opened one bleary eye and spoke: 'Back off. Go away. I'm about to have that vulture up there.'

Like that rooster, with Rod Steiger I have always felt that the best was yet to come. Keeping his pecker up, during good days and bad days, is what he is all about.

AFTERWORD

SONG OF INNOCENCE – AND EXPERIENCE

In the same way that I don't believe anybody sets out to make a bad movie – it just falls apart when the film-makers are not looking – so nobody believes their marriage can fail. Certainly not Rod Steiger. After all, marriage is the legal capstone you set upon the structure of love you've spent years putting together. You've invested time and money and trust in a relationship. In Steiger's case he and his wife would re-enact their marriage ceremony every year to remind themselves of their vows.

It seemed to me that the bond between Steiger and Paula, his fourth wife, was one of those Hollywood uniques. I thought it was a marriage made in durable heaven.

But, after all those years of togetherness, it was not to be. When Steiger rang to tell me that he and Paula were parting his voice was, surprisingly, not at all tearful: it was wan and faded as though he had wept all sorrow out of himself. When we met in London a few weeks later I felt he had been scoured of all recrimination.

I soon found out that the settlement and legal costs were hefty enough to provide the budget for a Third World country. But he was grateful to Paula, he said. 'After all, she was with me during the bad days of deep depression. She tended me. Now it is time to move on.' Which was more than my wife and I could do, because we had liked Paula; she had seemed to be good for our friend. It took a lot of getting used to.

Steiger let her and young Michael Winston stay on at his Malibu home for a couple of months so that the boy could enjoy Hallowe'en and Christmas there, in the place he was used to.

And Steiger and Paula were to share Michael fifty-fifty. That was important to Steiger, because it meant he still had a family. It was a share-and-share-alike of the child he loved by the woman he used to love.

That the end of his marriage was a traumatic disappointment which might easily flip him over again into the depressive dark side, which he had endured in the past, was something I feared. But Rod Steiger had grown stronger through the years.

So we jollied and joked during his stay in London and he seemed much like the early, ebullient Steiger with whom I had first become friends. 'You're taking it all very well,' I said.

He looked at me. 'You have to. You have to roll with the punches. Didn't you once call me a survivor? Well, I suppose that is really what I am: a survivor.

'And, anyway, I've spent a life in an occupation I love and I have a son and daughter whom I love. Disappointment is the price you pay and you ought to be willing to hand over. And, no, you mustn't cut her out of your book. After all, she is part of it as she was part of me.'

My wife always likes being hugged by Steiger. 'It's such a warm, comforting embrace.' I like that bear-hug, too. I hugged him extra hard when we parted this last time. If I'd had one I'd have given him an Oscar for taking it so well. After all, the real Oscar awards are very like marriage: a ceremony which acknowledges the survival of the fittest.

But those who fall by the wayside and get up again deserve something, too. Rod Steiger deserves my trophy, at least.

Poems and Pieces by Rod Steiger

Poem

I want to die.
I don't want to move.
I have no feeling for movement.
    To be left alone
    To disappear.
    Not to be bothered with
        washing
        shaving
        talking
        walking
going to the bathroom.
        Just to get out of this tunnel
        and the heavy darkness
        cold and oily
        constantly pressing against my brain and
        being.
To feel the way that this scum grease tallow pushes against
   your sides.
Crushing you!!
You!!
dead eyed, grey faced
unshaven, dirty of body
empty of mind.

Acting!

What's so important about acting?

        the paralyzing fear of not remembering lines.

        projections
        images
        visions of failure.
They're watching,
I can feel them on my body –
I can feel their eyes all over my skin.

        it's time to act!

The crew is watching, thirty of them,
The director is watching.
My partner in the scene is WATCHING.
A rat in the corner of the studio is WATCHING!
        I won't be able to do it!
        I won't be able to remember.
        They're going to discover I'm inadequate
        I'm unable.

        I must not scream.

        I must not scream in front of them.
        I must stay.
        I must not
        I must not listen to my mind.
        I must not
        I must not run off the set.
        I must not run
        I must not run.

I know I'll break down
They'll find out I'm weak
They'll find out I'm in pain
Oh God!
What GOD?
I will break down
I'll look like a fool
An idiot.
They'll find out I can't act
Can't act
Can't act at all.

End of vision.

There is no way out

My mind is telling me
There is a way out.

You get a gun.

A nice cool gun
And then –

Wait

You mustn't leave a mess.

I'm worried
I'm worried about the mess I'll look like
The head half gone
The blood on the walls
the carpet
the flowers
and over the cat.

I don't want my loved ones to walk in on that.

         there is a way
         there is a way

I live by the beach
There's the waiting
ever moving relentless ocean.

         I'll get a small rowboat
         while my wife's in town doing business
My daughter is in Europe, she won't know till later.
         I row out on the ocean
         I lower myself over the side of the boat
         holding tightly with my right hand
         to the boat.
         Keeping my head and shoulders above water
         holding with my left hand
         the gun
         pointing towards God's sky.
         Then
         I lower the gun
         taking the barrel in my mouth
         and
         pull the trigger.

Then I rest
I rest
I rest.

         The boat floats away
         My body floats away from it
         No mess
         No mess
         Fish food.

Strange
I'm more worried about the mess
          than
          my
          life.
I rest.
I rest.

          there is a way.

I don't like myself
I don't like myself.

          Fat
          Balding
          Old age.
          I hate the signs of age
          I hate it.

The deteriorating body
The thickening of limbs
stomach and face
The dry shedding of dead skin.

          I resent age
          I hate age
          I spit on age.
My narcissism screams at the victory of age
its progress
its ever present cruelty
in the mirror.
          I hate it.

          My wife Paula
          My poor wife Paula

Who
through eight years of my twisting freezing fog
heroically
kept my head above the waters of insanity
> Tending me like a crippled child
> Never criticizing me
> Never
> Never.

Never
In frustration
raised her voice
shouted or screamed
with the fury that comes with the fear of the unknown.
Never has she
tearfully begged
or demanded
her release or relief
saying
> 'How can you sit there like that!'
> 'What's wrong with you!'
> 'What kind of man are you!'
> 'How can you let yourself look like that!'

Never

> Always
> with the never ending stretching of patience
> kindness
> motherhood and maternity
> she more than gently
> took care of me.

Never
Never
Never reminded me

of my illness
My disease
My
'chemical imbalance'
       Isn't that the phrase that doctors use?

That love
That patience
That preserving shield
kept me from suicide
More than once.

       I sit in the squalor of myself.

Movement is my enemy
I sit staring at the sea
the sun
I sit
numb
Drowning in self-pity.
Maybe I'll die.
       Oh
       what if I die?

Let me not linger
Let it not be a long stretch of dying
Let me not linger
       let me
       in the depth of my depressive sleep
       never ending
       let me
       in that darkness
       depart.
       Let me die
       simply

173

not wake up.
That's exciting.
That's a goal
That would be an accomplishment

Once again
I feel the cold sheets of fear
moving about my body.
If I don't move
If I don't breathe
Maybe
They'll absorb me
and
bind me in a never ending
sleep
sleep.

I rest.
I rest.

Love

Perhaps because we are ever changing as humans we can never really get to know the complete entity of one another or ourselves, but, I believe the action of evolving creates a bond when the two people involved need the 'safety' of a true love, where the meeting of strangers bursts into a union of the gathering of the pain of the past – and through the exchange of what was denied them in the past – and what they unconsciously 'supply' each other – maybe the missing pieces of the complete heart – and that continuous exchange becomes the ever strengthening cement of their relationship and they grow through the fires of experience, and they create their own individual unique love. It is theirs, no one else's, and it is the true place of passionate peace.

ROD STEIGER
1997

For Anna Steiger
Room 486   Feb. 13, 1997

Dear Anna,
          courage can be present
          for an instant –
          heroes for a second –
          but –
          to battle fears and longings
          through the years
          with the sword of silence
          is to be truly heroic.

          To stand up to the unbearable foe –
          the devastating attacks
          of unhappy thoughts
          and destructive doubts –
          that
          is truly courageous.

          I am so proud your flag
          is always flying
          sighted eternally above
          the battle –
          passionate and indestructible.

          I love you deeply
          and devotedly
          now and always.

          forever Papa.
          Happy Birthday!

176

The *Guardian* Interview with Rod Steiger at the National Film Theatre, 23 August 1992

T.H.: This week the *Guardian*, who will be sponsoring the lecture – interview rather – said that Hollywood had forgotten Rod Steiger, which seems a strange way to reassure an interviewee. I think by that reception, Rod, you realize that we haven't forgotten you and we still pay you honour and tribute for giving us such marvellous moments of dramatic insight and entertainment.

R.S.: Thank you very much. It's really difficult for me to go on because Simon Callow's in the audience and he cut one of my scenes out of *The Ballad of the Sad Café*. Would you stand up, Mr Callow? [audience laughs and applauds] Thank you, Mr Callow. Also, you're fired, Mr Callow! [more laughs]

I thank everybody for being here and I am happy to say that, I have not felt forgotten, by the general public, in the many countries of the world where they have been fortunate enough for me to work and try to create something, and I thank you now, and I'll thank you at the end again for taking this time of your life and coming out . . . and we'll spend a little hour or two, and if I start to talk too much we may be here for breakfast. [laughs – Rod and audience] So go ahead.

T.H.: *Breakfast of Champions*, I'm allowed to say, you know. The . . . clips we saw just then of the taxi-cab scene. Which I believe you are rather fed up with now, aren't you?

R.S.: Well, I am in a way because . . . I guess it's the only thing they ever show. Well, I must . . . no I have to be honest about that scene . . . it's very interesting because we shot that scene in a studio, I think the studio was about the width of a rich lady's walk-in closet – you know, the size of it. When we got there, we couldn't believe it because they had half a taxi-cab, you know. And the front you never saw. And to make room they had half a cab and the guy sat driving it. You saw him. You saw the wheel and then you saw Mr Brando and myself. And I was a nervous wreck because I was going to . . . I'm playing Brando's brother, and Brando at that time had just established himself as one of the new gods of the American theatre and in the acting world. And I was very nervous about the whole thing. I remember I walked in and there was Sam Spiegel. Now Sam Spiegel was a great film producer, you know, and he talked like that [mimics accent] to Gadge. 'You know, Gadge,' he said. 'What's wrong with you, Gadge!'

T.H.: Gadge of course was Kazan.

R.S.: Gadge was Kazan's nickname. Elia Kazan, the director of *Waterfront*. And Kazan said: 'You son of a gun. You promised me we would have a backdrop so when we shoot at the two actors in the cab through the window in the back we see the streets of New York, and you haven't delivered it. And I can't shoot this damned thing unless there's a backdrop.' And he said: 'Gadge, you shouldn't get excited, so excited I can't shoot the scene.'

One of the members of the crew said: 'You know, Mr Kazan, when I came to work this morning there was a venetian blind in the back window of the cab.' And Kazan, being no idiot, said: 'Get me a venetian blind as fast as you can.' Right? Now the interesting thing is they put the venetian blind in. But because of the cheapness of the studio, the small studio we were in, if you put your hand out of the window here, you could touch the wall. And that means he couldn't shoot from the side over somebody's shoulder too much like he'd like to. That means he was forced to go in on the actors. And what happens is that actors are human beings before they're actors, and we were nervous enough. And now we had a feeling it was all up to us, and it added a special tension. Beside the fact that Kazan in his sadistic way was very keen to see, as he called, 'the two young bulls lock horns in this scene', right? 'Cos he knew we would kill each other if the other shouldn't come out too much better than the other one, right? [laughs – audience and interviewer].

T.H.: What about that thing with Marlon Brando pressing down the gun? I mean, that's a thing nobody would ever do, or dare to do in real life, isn't it?

R.S.: Well, I know that if a director came to me and said: 'Now when your brother takes out the gun you just say "no, don't be ridiculous".' I'd say: 'What the hell's wrong with . . . the hell. He'd shoot me . . . what are you saying "don't be"?' You know. What happened was that Brando . . . somebody had talked to him and had told a story about a relative pulling a gun, and a guy had pushed the gun round and said, "Charlie, take it easy". Well, maybe not Charlie, but that was his name. And that was to me the most creative scene in the film. When Brando just pushed the gun aside. And the audience accepted it. You know, that was exciting and I . . . Anyway, that's part of the history of that scene.

T.H.: How did you get on with Brando actually?

179

R.S.: I never got to know him very well.

T.H.: You refer to him still as *Mr* Brando I noticed.

R.S.: It depends what day it is. [audience laughs] Yeah, well, I have a new thing, I guess because I'm sixty-seven and I got older and I got a new thing which is, anybody who does sixty per cent good work and lasts more than twenty years you have to call him Mr in my business, you know. I consider myself sixty per cent virgin and forty per cent whore, you know. And the whore's part is when you did pictures you didn't want to do because you were trying to establish yourself, or you were in debt, or you were trying to pay off an alimony or mortgage on the house. And you substituted your artistic beliefs for your monetary necessities, you know. But no, the last time I heard from him he sent me a telegram saying let's be friends so we can help the Indians. [R.S. and audience laugh]

T.H.: Did you send a reply?

R.S.: I filed it in the wastebasket. [laughs] I did say something though, even though I was angry, 'cos he left me during part of the scene to go and see a psychiatrist and I was sitting here by myself. I really don't get the childish sense of revenge that I used to get and I'm reluctant to go into any detail because of the tragedies that have struck this man's life, with his daughter and his son being stuck on a murder charge and that. So my little harping seems childish and ridiculous.

T.H.: How did you respond to Kazan's treatment of you? I mean, you described him as a sadist. How did that work?

R.S.: I don't understand the sadist part of your question.

180

T.H.: You mention sadist. That he'd been a sadist. He wanted two young bulls . . .

R.S.: Ah. Kazan would do anything to get a result in a scene. Anything. There is a scene in the picture where we are sitting around a table, a pool table, and we're getting the money back from various gangsters and I'm with the lawyer/ book-keeper what have you, and Lee J. Cobb, a fantastic actor, was in the scene playing the head of the mob, or the mafia, whatever it was, and I kept hearing Kazan walk by. Cobb would be here and he'd walk by Cobb and say: 'Get him', you know. And I didn't know what he was talking about. And then he'd come by me and say: 'Kill him', right? [audience laugh] 'Get him'. And I'm being very quiet 'cos I'm glad I'm in the picture. [everyone laughs]

But what happens is that this young actor who is supposed to be a man who's caught cheating by having money in his coat, they think they won't search him. Well, this actor came in and they did the lines. All of a sudden Lee J. Cobb picks him up by the lapels, slams him on his back on top of the pool table, rips the inside of the lining of his coat, takes out the money, slaps it in his face, picks him up and kicks him in the ass off the set. Now I knew what 'Get him' meant. [laughs] Now I knew. I don't do 'Get him' scenes any more. [everyone laughs] Anyway, he would do anything. He would do anything. But I'm gonna have to tell you something else.

One of the things about that picture which is interesting is that it might have had one of the best casts of any picture at that time, but besides that, everyone in that picture, the majority of the feature roles were members of the Actors' Studio. That was the organization that showed Crawford as producer in New York and Bobby Lewis as director. And Kazan formed a unit that got the best actors in New York theatre to have a place to rehearse. You see, because the terrible thing about being an actor is, in my country there's

181

no place you can take a chance, or there was no place you could take a chance of freeing yourself from the fear of making a mistake. And the Actors' Studio came along and you could be as hammy and as bad as you liked, but you learned and you weren't fired from the production, which would happen to you in the commercial world. So it didn't have the arts and crafty thing about it that it has today.

It was a smart move by producers to get the best actors together so when they cast the play they could get the actors, and when they cast the movies we get the actors. And this is my long-winded way of saying everybody knew each other and had a common principle in their acting. A common way of searching for the elusive, unproven, the provable thing – THERE YOU ARE! [audience laughs] Jesus Christ I thought I was alone! [everyone laughs] Really, I thought we were getting ready for bed though. I swear. Anyway, you will be here for the night so you might as well relax, you know. Anyway what happened was that we all knew each other and had one way of working and that helped a great deal.

T.H.: That kind of method approach, doesn't it put the backs up of other directors, Rod?

R.S.: I don't like the word Method. I don't mean that you said it, but I don't, but I . . . What happened was that there was a generation of actors. For many years the American actor did what he thought the character would do in the scene. Then there was the group theatre, that was in the thirties and beginning of the forties. Excuse me. I take a medicine and if my mouth dries out I'm dead, right?

Anyway, so what happened was that they went and . . . the Moscow, that is the Moscow theatre outside the communist . . . ? came back saying 'Stanislavsky the great teacher of theatre in Moscow does this, does that. You're supposed to do it as if it was happening to YOU'. And then the American actor, the *new* American actor begins to say: 'It's not just a mother dying. The man's mother dying as it appears in the script. It is *my* mother dying.'

So what we were looking for was the individual reaction which would be different in any person in the world, because no two people relate to any relative or friend in the same way. And that's what we were looking for. Like I say in the role of poetry, your voice, I mean your speaking voice, even that comes out. I mean one of the highest compliments I get in my life today is when somebody says, I'm on a subway and somebody says, I'm on an elevator and nobody recognizes me until I talk to my wife or something and then they look and look again, and they recognize my voice. Now why that's a compliment is that I'm involved personally.

You see the young actor when he starts out, he comes on stage and he says: 'Good morning how are you?' [puts on 'English' voice – all laugh] And all he is worried about is how he looks, right? Then he talks with this voice, and his mother when he goes home that night says: 'What the hell was wrong with you? You had a frog in your throat?' [all laugh] Right? What's wrong with you? And I remember the first time when I was acting a scene, and I was saying: 'Now look, Gordon, we gotta do something about this. There's something terribly wrong here and I want to tell you something else, I don't like you,' in my voice, finally it took me two years. I was talking with my own voice. There's better voices, there's worse voices, but it was me, in the scene worried about the circumstances, fictitious as they may be, as if they were happening to me. It is my brother I'd pulled the gun on in the back of the cab. And when I'd pulled the gun, after that he'd pushed the gun away. All I want to do, I don't know if you see the scene again, I don't move because all I could think was: 'Jesus. It's my brother. And let me evaporate. If I stay still I'll disappear in this cab.' It didn't happen, you know, so I'd shown that, you know, so . . . and then that acting spread around the world now. Spread around the world more personal. Mr Albert Finney. Mr Tom Courtenay. Tom Conti and all the other younger, wonderful actors that you have, you know . . . and that's the end of that.

T.H.: But do you not feel that there are some directors, I mean, there are directors such as Hitchcock or Antonioni who wouldn't allow that kind of experimentation?

R.S.: I improvise a great deal, and I paraphrase a great deal. I don't put my fellow actors into a state of alarm, because I always make sure that the last word or two is the cue that he is supposed to get. I have worked with actors who try to improvise, you know, and they all of a sudden are calling you Schwartz and your name is Smith [audience laughs], and . . . I'll tell you a funny story, talking about improvising. We started to shoot the taxi scene and Marlon said to me: 'How's ma?' – that's not the script, right? I said: 'I don't know,' and he said, 'Well, how do you think she's feeling?' [audience laughs] So I said, 'I don't know,' and the improvisation is sometimes really having the guts to do what you think according to the situation that you're in. So I said: 'I don't know what you're asking me about ma for. She's your mother. You take a dime. You put it in the phone. You dial our phone number and say, "Hello, ma, how are you?".' And they said 'CUT'. [everyone laughs] Now we start again and he says: 'What do you think of the Yankees?'

T.H.: Was he trying to throw you, Rod?

R.S.: I wouldn't say that. [everyone laughs] Anyway. He said, 'What do you think of the Yankees?'
I said: 'I don't understand you today. I don't understand what you're doing. I mean, we live in Brooklyn. We were brought up in Brooklyn. Our father used to drag us until our

184

asses were tired to the Brooklyn Dodgers game, and you keep asking me how the Yankees are!' – 'CUT'. [everyone laughs] It took us eleven hours. [more laughs] That's true.

T.H.: How does that work in the commercial . . . when you're allowed that?

R.S.: An actor gets to be like a racehorse. In any profession – forget acting, shmacting, it's not that important. What is important is you, through your record, through your contribution, through your nerve, through your courage, try to make dreams for other people to understand and feel, and if you're fairly successful you'll get a record, as a whole. If you're a good runner.

And the director, if he's good enough, lucky enough to get a bunch of actors like that, will have established that you are reliable. And what they do is, I mean the best I've worked with, except those who cut your theme [everyone laughs] . . . Mr Callow! Anyway, so what happens is they give you the set. I mean working with a man like Sidney Lumet or Elia Kazan, they're very . . . I'll explain the difference in directors in a minute, they're very good because they've been actors you see. You've earned the right, and I said Mr Kazan or Mr Lumet, 'What do you want, what do you want to do?' He says: 'There it is, go ahead.' Then you do the scene with the other actors and he's there with the cameraman and you can hear him whisper: 'We'll do a close on that. I like that. We'll do it freer than that. Let's go back to the . . .'

And I think it's the only way really for directing in movies. Out of the actors and the director's discovery of the scene, what is photographed is born, rather than being superimposed by some idea. The director comes in . . . I think it was Antonioni drew chalk lines on the floor before you'd even got there to go to work. I could never work with a director like that. I'd kill him. I'd say what's the . . . how do I know how

185

I'm going to walk there? I don't understand what you're talking about. But that's because strange things can happen in a movie. Strange things happen.

During the war, they lost a lot of their actors, and were left with older actors and then the real theatre of Italy is opera. So what happened was they took people off the street and rather than being bicycle people, all these wonderful things, and . . . they drew chalk lines because they weren't actors. And then, they dubbed the actor's voice. These people couldn't speak or act right, but they looked right. Their image was great. Then, from the little theatre of Milan – that was one of them – and another theatre company, months later, the good theatre actor would come in and put in the voice of the character in the bicycle scene. There's another person's voice. That's what they were forced to do, you know.

I could never work . . . I have to be . . . left alone. And that's the way with Kazan and Lumet. Sometimes you get in trouble. And I will tell you, how I got in trouble. I was once working with a wonderful, great, incredible, intellectual, educated, I don't know how compassionate, director named David Lean. And Mr Lean, and he earned it every step of the way, was a god to his crew and his people. And in comes this idiot of an American, right? And all I'm thinking is, 'my God! Alec Guinness, Ralph Richardson. If I have any good speech left in my body let it come out now! [everyone laughs] Please. God. I don't want the crew to be reduced and say you're sorry. You know he's saying 33rd and 4th street, that's right.' [more laughs] Anyway, the first night of shooting. It's a nice shot and there's a scene. And the camera's here, and they lay down tracks and the camera goes on the tracks. And my lady actress and I are sitting in the sleigh, and all it is, that we pass the camera, I kiss her. She is surprised and shocked, and maybe a bit titillated, I don't know. And we move on. Well, our lady was anticipating the kiss. In acting the body gives it away. She was in . . . she'd read the script, and you know [more laughs] So we did a couple of these things and then I said . . . I'll never forget. You talk about a man hanging himself. I said: 'I've got an idea, Mr Lean'. [R.S. laughs – audience laughs] He said, with a cigarette: 'Oh do you!' [everyone laughs] 'And what kind of an idea exactly is it?' [mimics Mr Lean laughing – audience laughs] So I said: 'Well, if we lay down a little more track, so we go past the camera and we have a little more track and you go with us. I'll kiss her once, she'll figure that's it and she'll be relaxed like you want and I'll put a yard of tongue down her throat.' [audience laughs] He said: 'Ah.' We did it, and the actress relaxed and then I put a yard of tongue down her throat, and [he gasps] she was like that, and that was it! I was never forgiven for that. And Mr Lean I don't think ever liked me for that. I was nice. I took him aside and then said . . . you know.

Mr Lean was one of the greatest, I've been so lucky. I've worked with Zinnemann, and Kazan and Lumet and David Lean and people like that. The thing about Zhivago I liked is that American actors were getting a little angry 'cos the American producer in the theatre and in films double-crossed them. By that I mean that when they got anything with style, they brought over the English actor. Which is fine. There are good and bad actors in each country. But the English actor they also brought over because the English actor at that time was uninformed and was taking much less money. [audience laughs] No. I mean it's a terrible thing they were doing. Much less money than the American actor did. Now the English actors are pretty shrewd, now they've caught up, right? And it got to be that if there was anything of style the American actor couldn't do it, 'Get an English actor'. And I was happy that I came off pretty even in the film. And so say, 'Yes, American actors, if you give us a chance we can speak well, we can move well, etc.' But that's the thing that made me feel best about that.

T.H.: What about working with somebody as distanced from the actor as Chabrol, you know, you worked with him?

R.S.: It was one of the worst experiences of my life. [audience laughs] Well, what happened with that picture was I got all excited. They said Chabrol would be interested in working. I said: 'Oh my God! Yes I want to get into the French industry because I think better material is in Europe, England, France, in all those places.' I thought that's wonderful. Romy Schneider was in the picture, one of the most nervous women, God help her. And she killed herself. Anyway, and I get there and they have a young Italian in the lead. I don't know how to describe this person, right? This man would have trouble sneezing. [audience laughs] I mean, just a natural sneeze, never mind anything to do with the play or the movie, right? However, he was very good at doing the hair right, and looking good, and Chabrol had realized he had made a mistake, and then out came the fatal symbol – a chess set. Now follow this. Chabrol would be in the next room playing chess, while the cameraman and his crew who he'd had for twenty years set up the shots and when they said, 'We're ready,' Chabrol would probably say, 'Checkmate. I'll be back in a minute, I'm doing a movie over here,' and we'd come in and shoot the scene, and there was no communication . . . he had given up, I think, on the picture. It was a disaster. Just one of those terrible things that happen sometimes, you get somebody in a principal role and you're finished. And for some reason or other they don't replace them. I don't know why.

T.H.: You have in fact assisted, if I may put it that way, with direction of some British films I've seen you on. I was thinking of *Across the Bridge*, for instance. You've never actually officially directed a film though, have you? Would you like to have done?

188

R.S.: I couldn't . . . Yeah, I would like to do it, 'cos I've helped out a bit when . . . you see I have a kind of a . . . you have to take what applies to your life and to your profession and . . . I think that if you offer to help somebody three times and the third time they still look at you like you're an idiot, then I come in and play my part, then I go home. That's it. I'm not trying to take over, you know. I've had this discussion with people. I'm not trying to take over your picture, I just wanted to get the kiss right, and you know . . .

T.H.: Did you have this problem with Simon Callow?

R.S.: No, absolutely no. No, Simon was playing draughts. [audience laughs] Anyway, no I re-wrote *Al Capone*. I didn't want to do *Al Capone*, I was on my high, you know, when you're young, your philosophy is as good as your health. Don't think that's a joke. When you feel good, and you've got bread in the house, and somebody who loves you. That's why I turned down *Patton*. I had got the Academy award. There I was on top of the world for three seconds. That's the time it takes to hand you the statue. For those three seconds you are the most important actor in the world. After those three seconds it starts to go down. [audience laughs] Until you get another hit. And if you don't get another hit, it goes down . . . it goes down further.

T.H.: Why didn't you take *Patton*, Rod?

R.S.: Well, I was very young, and as I say, cocky, and I was always a pacifist. I didn't believe in war, and they just hit me on the right day, when I said, 'I can't do this. I'm not going to glorify a general,' you know. If I'd had no money in the house and no food, I would have got on my knees and begged them, 'Please let me do *Patton*,' you know. But I was healthy and well provided for by myself. And if I had done it,

I think if I had done it half as good as Mr Scott, and got a nomination, I might have had a chance to sneak into *The Godfather*. That's how the business goes. I still would have been hot. That terrible word 'hot'. I've had ten years, eight years of depression. I am not hot any more. And I have the pleasure now of opening newspapers and reading words next to me, they put the word 'forgotten', which cheers you up. [audience laughs] Really makes you feel like you belong. But that's all right because the game's afoot, you know, and our flag is flying. And I have not been forgotten. I know I haven't been forgotten because this house is a full house, you see.

When I was young and I heard about these occasions. We don't have this in America, really. One of the reasons why I've always felt like a misplaced European is because of the respect there is for the arts in England and Europe. We don't . . . It's not even in our school system. We get introduced to Shakespeare . . . you walk in the class when you're about eight years of age and there's a book called *Julius Caesar*, and somebody is saying 'thee, thou and though' and 'the russet hills', and we're saying, 'What's that?' You see a production at eight or nine. Your childish mind says, 'What's that? Oh, look at that. Oh, what nice words. Oh. It's the *theatre*!' And you grow up with it. We don't get that, you know. That's why I always said I think you're the most rounded English speaking performers, because often your cinema and your theatre are in the same city. What happens to an actor like me . . . this is a true story. You get successful in the theatre or you do a show like *Marty* on television which changed my life in the United States. You get to Hollywood and you start doing all sorts of pictures. You're very hot. I did nine pictures in a row without ten days off between them, because I refused to sign with a studio. I wanted . . . I was a man . . . I'll tell you another story about that. I refused to sign with a studio, and I'll never forget that.

Anyway, my point was you're in Hollywood, you're

190

comfortable, you're doing scenes four minutes length, three minutes, maybe seven minutes. Your span of concentration, your demand is shorter. You're there about four or five years and they send you this huge book . . . and it's called a play. And you get the play! I have to concentrate for two hours. [audience laughs] I haven't done that in seven years! And you don't do it. And you cut your throat in half. And you begin to become a coward. Then finally, as you get near the middle of your career, now you get angry – this is what happened to me and they said, 'What about doing a play called *Rashomon*, based upon the movie *Rashomon*.' And at that I said, 'I gotta go.' I have an expression – I gotta go means I have to do something – not to the bathroom all the time, right? I have to go. I have to do this because I believe in the theatre, and the theatre I like is the theatre that you can't turn on on television and you can't quite get in the movies. It is a personal communication in one given room called an auditorium where there is a little bit of the circus from whence the theatre came, and a little bit of the magic of storytelling from whence theatre came, and *Rashomon* had that, like *Madame Butterfly* had that, and like plays . . . And I also believe that now the public in general unconsciously, at least in my country, with television and what have you, and movies constantly hitting you with realism and realism. They're getting a little weary. Now you come along with a crazy picture like *The Fisher King*, which has got a little fairy tale in it, and I watched the audience. They loved it. Because you must never leave out the little bit of child that's in the most mature person in the audience. You have to have an excitement about it. You can't just can it, and you can't just snap it on television. And that was a success.

Then I did *Moby Dick*, by Orson Welles. There's nothing wrong with my ego, right? *Moby Dick* by Orson Welles, this is what you have to do. It's a simple chore. You make your entrance running down the middle of the theatre. You come

up on stage and you do a scene from *King Lear* with Cordelia.
The next thing you do in the next act . . . then you stop . . .
'No. No, no, darling. No, no, I have found something
wonderful. Something called *Moby Dick'*. And that's what
we're going to do and they rehearse *Moby Dick*. Then you
have to do the father speech which goes on for seven to
twelve minutes. Right? And in the last act, having nothing
else to do, you pretend you're limp and your name is Ahab.
[audience laughs] I want to tell you that I had . . . on
matinées a very intellectual performance. It wasn't very
emotional on matinées because I said . . . I don't believe an
actor should do eight performances in the theatre. I mean, I
believe the ideal theatre's repertory which we all know,
because, I mean . . . there's another thing I'll never
understand. I have people in my country who have done the
same television show for TWENTY-TWO YEARS. The actor's
dead. Obviously he died somewhere after the third year.
[audience laughs] No. He's dead. His growth and his
development, that's another thing I hate. In my country, you
have a young talent. He comes along . . . well, I'll tell you
how to sum it up. I have young actors coming up to me and
saying 'How do I become a television star?' I say, 'Very
simple, you grow a tail, two more legs and call yourself
Lassie.' [audience laughs] Then they get into the television
medium which gives no time for rehearsal. And rehearsal is
the most important part of creating for an actor. No time. So,
unconsciously, the actor's forced to fall back on clichés and
things like that. Though he doesn't know it, piles bad habit
after bad habit on himself. The success of the series he's in
ends in about four years, and he's forgotten like that. And his
talent has been crippled. And you read in the papers, 'So and
so. Drug addict. So and so. Alcoholic'. You know. I don't
know how I got into that, but that is what happens.

T.H.: What was the question? [audience laughs] You've just

192

done a TV movie yourself. Was that the same sort of grind for you?

R.S.: Not for me. No. You mean the *Frank Sinatra Story*?

T.H.: Yeah. 'Cos at last you got a chance to play a Godfather.

R.S.: No. I did. I played Sam Giancana. It was a cameo. I had two scenes on a golf course and one in a night-club. And I'm the fattest Sam Giancana that ever lived. He weighed about a hundred and forty-two pounds, and I'm playing him, like, you know. Anyway, let us move on.

T.H.: What about the past? In fact, Rod, you mention direction, but in something like *Across the Bridge*, I remember that the director then was not at all happy with some of your suggestions, but you still pursued him.

R.S.: Well now, to me the basis of my work – and I guess the basis of any human being's life – should be preservation and the defence of logic. In this script, *Across the Bridge*, there's this very rich multimillionaire, German millionaire. They're catching up to him. Scotland Yard. He tries to get to Mexico, where he's got a million dollars in a bank, and he gets stuck in a small town, and this dog befriends him, and pretty soon he degenerates. The chief of police in the town wants the money he's got in the bank. The German is too obstinate. He won't do it. He then becomes like a homeless bum. And then . . . but he falls in love with the dog. And they tie the dog on the bridge. *Across the Bridge* was the name of the picture. And there's a line across the bridge. That's one side's the United States, one side's Mexico. The authorities have to get him on the other side where it says United States, 'cos then they can arrest him. So they tie the dog over there, and he has fallen in love with the dog, and they sleep under the bridge with

193

the garbage and everything and that night they have this scene [makes emotional noises] and he finally goes to get the dog and he unties it on the American side and cars come rushing towards him. He tries to run but he falls down and gets killed by the car. And that's the end of the picture. My question was, if this man paid no attention to human beings, why did he pay attention to this dog? The directors are ridiculous. 'It's the script. It's the script.' I said, 'I know it's the script. I can feel it's the script. It's in my hand. Why does he pay attention to this dog? If he treats everybody else like crap.' He said, 'But what should the dog do? Save his life or something?' I said, 'Yes. Maybe.' And all of a sudden, there's a scene in the picture where he gets on a bus leading out of the Mexican town, they catch him, take him out, and he walks back through the desert. And I said, 'OK. He walks back through the desert. He gets tired from the heat. He lies down and he falls asleep.' The dog has followed him all this way 'cos the dog loves him, and the dog is barking and wakes him up, and he's German and he says *Was ist das?'* at the dog. And he sees the dog keeps barking, and on his left leg is a tarantula. Then he knocks it off with his hat, and he steps on it and looks around 'cos I found that they always travel in pairs [audience and R.S. laugh] and he kills that, and then knowing a little bit about drama, he starts to walk away . . . and I feel the audience is now saying, 'Oh, come on, you can't walk away, this dog saved your life:' [R.S. and audience laugh] and he walks away. Then he stops and says, '*Liebchen.* *Liebchen*, come here. *Liebchen*. Come here, love.' And that's how they became friends. So that's how I get in trouble with directors sometimes, 'cos I say, 'Why does he pay attention to the dog?' And there are a lot of directors, especially people who are cameramen, and people who are technicians of some sort, who become directors, who are marvellous at assembling, putting a picture together, but they . . . if the actor's in trouble, they don't know what to do. They'll give

you a result term. They'll say we want it to be faster here. I
don't know how to get up and act faster. Angry here. And
that's why like Kazan and those people are the best people
I've ever worked with, 'cos those people, they were actors.
But that's how I got in trouble all my life, even when I did
live television. I got in more trouble saying 'why?' you know.
But then again, it helped whatever I am today. I eat much
better. I live much better. And I got a beautiful wife. And
maybe part of the reason is because I say WHY, I WANNA
KNOW WHY. [raises voice] I don't want to look like an idiot.

T.H.: Which of your roles would you like to go back and
re-do?

R.S.: *W. C. Fields.* I'm gonna sound like the biggest gossip in
the world. 'Cos there were people in the cast who were
mixed up on alcohol and dope, and I had to do my part with
the director reading me their lines while they were
unconscious upstairs, in the house we were shooting in. And
acting is basically reacting, and if you don't have the other
actor there, then you're playing the scene like there was no
camera, it's not easy to get an honest comfortable
performance, you know. What I'd like to do in the future is
the last days of Beethoven, the problem with him and his
nephew and the mother, and Einstein, you know, things that
would fit my age. I think with a little make-up – a lot of
make-up – what am I talking a little make-up! A lot of
make-up – I could do the last days of Hemingway. You know,
like a television special or something. I would like to do that.
If I had had my way. I never signed with a major studio.

T.H.: Why was that? Why didn't you?

R.S.: Well, I'll tell you a story that makes it clear. Have you
got a minute? [audience laughs]

195

I'll tell you this story. I did *Marty*. I want to explain to the people in the audience, being primarily English. *Marty* was a television show that, along with a lot of fine people, changed American television one night out of three hundred and sixty-five days. It was on one hour and they started to do in America after then *A Slice of Life*. The story of a butcher. You saw the movie, I'm sure. The butcher. The lonely butcher in the Bronx. All he wants to do is learn how to love, or not to be lonely. And he did it, and . . . I knew he had done . . . see, an actor knows in his stomach when he's doing something good. If you meet an actor who knows in his stomach he is doing something great, fire that sort of a bitch 'cos he's an egotist, he doesn't know what he's doing. Right? Greatness is an accident. To me a great person is a person who takes two known thoughts, puts them together and you have a new thought in the world. That's as far as we can go, folks, as human beings. You see, Jesus, he took an orange and took an apple and put it together and it's something you've never seen but you can eat it, and it smells . . . and it's something new in the world. Anyway. So we did the show. I went home. I got up. I came downstairs – I was living in a five dollar a week room, and I was going to my little café to get my corn muffin and a cup of tea. And I started to walk down the street and a garbage truck went by, and the garbage man said, 'Hey Marty! What are you doing tonight, Marty? Where are you going to go?' That was a scene. Those lines were very important in the play, and I came back to that with my cue. I said, 'I don't know. Where do you want to go?' Right. A woman passes me on the street and says 'What we gonna do tonight, Marty?' and I begin to say, 'Jesus Christ. Something's happened here.' Then I get into the café, the little shop and the guy says, 'Hey Marty. What we gonna do tonight?' I said, 'I don't know. What do you wanna do tonight, I don't know what, I don't know.' [audience laughs]

Anyway. This was the closest thing to my heart, this part,

'cos I never liked playing villains, you see. I have great luck. But one of the shadowy parts of my luck was when I did Jud in *Oklahoma!* As far as Hollywood was concerned I was a villain from then on, because I have some strength and some power. The more ruthless, the more powerful, the more happy they got. So I get a phone call, they said Burt Lancaster and Harold Hecht had bought *Marty*. They're gonna do it as a picture. I get this call from Paddy Chayefsky. I said, 'Oh, great. If we all stick together, we'll do this picture', and one thing leads to another and they call me up in the office. And this is why I never signed the contract. I know it's a long-winded story. I get up there . . . I don't have short-winded stories. [audience laughs] Anyway. I get up there and there I'm sitting, and I'm nervous as can be and they say, and I love that, 'You know we're doing a film of *Marty* don't you?' I said, 'I've heard a rumour, yes.' He said, 'Well, we'd like you to play Marty.' I felt like saying, 'That's big of you', since I created him. [audience laughs] But I didn't say it. I said 'That's wonderful.' He said, 'But you may have to sign a seven-year contract.' I said, 'I don't believe in contracts.' I said, 'All right. Maybe to do Marty I'll sign a seven-year contract.' I said, 'But let me ask you a question. Who chooses my parts?' They said, 'We do.' I said, 'No you don't.' I have the right to sleep with whom I please. If I'm going to make a mistake, it's going to be something I chose. I chose. You must not take the right from any human being of choice. And I lost the picture. You know. But that's why I didn't sign the contract there. That'll answer your questions. [audience and I laugh]

T.H.: Did that make you angry, Rod? There's a lot of anger in you and in your performances, I've always thought.

R.S.: Well. That's another thing. I'll tell you that. Just another second. I'll have another glass of water and I'll tell you.

197

[audience laughs] What happened was that at nine years of age my family disappeared because of the problem of alcoholism. What happened was I was taking members of my family, my mother out of pubs. They called me, 'Come get your mother.' What happened was the children in the neighbourhood and the people in the neighbourhood, specially the children, would tease you, and we all know how children can hurt. Right? And we've hurt other people when we were children. And I think something happened in me that said, 'I'm gonna do something, someday. That nobody will laugh at the name of Steiger.' I'm talking from a psychiatric point of view now. I've learned this over the years. I'm not talking about how well or good I did it. I'm talking about why people say to me, 'Jesus, when you work, you work like you're gonna die if it doesn't work right.' And I said, 'Yeah. Maybe my name will.' You know. And so that anger, which I still have in me today, luckily I've found a place that could channel it in acting. But otherwise I know I would have probably become an alcoholic. I would have been the man that you see coming in the pub, you see. And everybody would be whispering, 'Let's get out the back door. This son of a bitch is going to pick a fight.' And I would pick the fight, and I would have been a nasty bastard. And finally some day, someone would shove a knife in my ribs, and it would have been over. But luckily, this anger, or whatever I have . . . I got into . . . I never wanted to be an actor. I never dreamed of being an actor.

I went in the Navy at sixteen and I came out when I was twenty-one. I didn't know what to do, but I believe a man is supposed to earn his bread, and not ask other people to do it, so I said, 'Well go to the civil service. They're taking veterans. Have priority.' So I went to the veterans priority. They took you. They took you even if you had the IQ of a decimal point. Right? [audience laughs] They took you . . . I was in the civil service . . . I'm making this as fast as I can. And I noticed on the floor that I worked, all of a sudden the fellas begin to check with each other and I said, 'What the hell is going on here? All the attractive girls are busy every third Thursday of the month. What's up?' So we snuck around . . . well, this is a huge organization of twelve thousand people. A block square building. They had organized a theatre group. Well, we came down like vultures on the theatre group, right? We wanted to get a hold of the women, right? So I went into the theatre group. I did two plays and the woman said, 'Well, I think you should take it seriously.' It shocked me. I never . . . Well, I said, 'What do you mean take it seriously? These are golden people. I never saw a play on the screen. If I was good, when my family was together I got a dime for taking out the garbage and drying the dishes and I'd go to the matinée and I'd see my Henry Wilcoxon and the Crusaders and stuff like that.' She said, 'No.' I said, 'And besides, I can't afford it.' And this is why I'm an actor. My government had a thing called the GI Bill of Rights. It paid for your schooling. I was a lazy slob and I said to myself, 'Well, hell. I'll make believe I'm an actor for four years. If that's what I get for each year of service. It's eighty-five dollars a month. I can live on that. And I'll be an actor. You know, a *bon vivant*.' [audience laughs] Anyway. So I went over and I auditioned. And I didn't get three words out. They said, 'Fresh. Interesting talent.' That's because they wanted the money from the government to keep the school running. [audience laughs] Right? And I said, 'Oh Mabel. Wonderful! Wonderful! Right? Right? Did you see. Oh my God! Mabel!' [audience laughs]

Now what happened was, it was the most fortunate accident for me as a human being. I fell in love with it. I'll show you how you follow it . . . all the way from a nine-year-old boy, I fell in love with the stage, I fell in love with it. Then I became fanatic, and then I must say . . . I made a bit of a mistake. I tried to make my life out of my

199

profession. And ladies and gentlemen, no matter what your
profession is you can't sleep with it, you can't kiss it, you
can't hold it. You just can't do it. And I went through three
marriages because of that. I was going to be the artist.
Unfettered. The art was first. My profession was first. Never
mind what you think of my wife, how do you like the play?
Right? And one day I remember I went to see an analyst, and
I said, 'I wanna be an . . . My dream is to be free in a
monetary society. To work with what I want to do. To get up
when I want to do. etc. etc. etc. And I don't want to be a
slave to all these things. And I don't want to be a slave to the
clock. To catching the bus. To getting to the office. I wanna be
free.' And he said these words and I pass them on to you, and
he said, 'My friend. You are a slave to freedom!' Oh. Oh.
[audience laughs] Boy was he right! Was he right. You can't
kiss a script goodnight. You just can't do it.

But the other part . . . I'm lucky because I belong to a
group of people who make a living at something they do . . .
when I was in my depression for eight years. Everybody
thought I was heroic or brave or were nice to me, my friends.
The only thing . . . that kept me alive was my wife. And I was
going to do away with myself, I had the gun . . . now I'll tell
you this is what I did. I shall just show you. It wasn't that I
was going to kill myself. I was worried about leaving a mess.
How's that for social conditioning? [audience laughs] I'm
worried my daughter, or Paula, my beloved wife, would see
the blood on the walls. So we live by the beach, I rent a boat,
a little row boat. I go out on the water. I lower myself,
holding with my right hand the side of the boat because I'm
left-handed, putting the revolver inside my mouth and
blowing my head off. The boat goes one way and I become
fish food. That's how far . . . and I was looking for a boat and
pricing them. Now I'm not asking for sympathy. But had I
not, at this late time of my life – who knows what time it is
in life but that's another discussion – at this time, whatever I

am now, been blessed with Paula, I wouldn't be boring the shit out of you now. [audience laughs] Would you stand up, Paula? [audience applauds]

I have to tell you an old man's secret, and I love it. I walk into a cocktail party. My wife when I met her was twenty. I was fifty-four, right? By the way, I'm having a child. Take that, Warren Beatty! [audience laughs and applauds] Let's see what *he* does at sixty-seven! [more laughs and applause] When he gets to be sixty-seven I'm sending him a telegram that says, 'Well?' [more laughs] Right?

Anyway . . . Paula . . . one of the great pleasures in my life is I walk into a party or something with Paula, and somebody comes up and says, 'Oh! is this your daughter Anna?' And the ego . . . the ego boosts like a rocket. I say, 'No. This is my wife who happens to be thirty-four years younger than I.' [audience laughs]

Anyway. I'm beginning to get warmed up.

T.H.: I gathered that. Rod, what caused the depression? Was it that the . . .

R.S.: I doubt if I could answer that. I have so many letters from people. I am now working with the head of the National Film Institute. They're all congratulatory. I'll tell you what makes a hero. It's very interesting. They say, 'My God. You're the only one – well not the only one – who's come down and done something who's known. You've come out of the closet and said that you were a depressed person.' And I thought, I don't know what you're talking about. Yeah! I'm depressed. But I'm ready to go bye. I'm going to go to Washington. I'm going to meet with congressmen and senators. I want the stigma taken off the pain that people have in their lives. [audience applauds] I don't want people to be damned because they have a mental disease, or they have schizophrenia, or they have alcoholism. It's part of life. And

201

no god, whoever you believed in, would sentence you because you feel pain, and I'm gonna fight it. [applause] Now where were we, between pain and depression? [audience laughs]

I had a by-pass operation. And they took veins from my legs and they put it around my heart, whatever you want to call it. And they said, you know, 'Be careful. You may go into a depression.' Never say that to an actor. [audience laughs] Jesus Christ, never suggest anything to an actor. I don't go into depressions, I disappear into swamps of agony. [audience laughs] Crawling back through endless tunnels of time. No bottom. Right? Well, I went in it for four years. And I'm talking about depression. I'm not talking about me feeling blue for a couple of months. I'm talking about not washing, not bathing and sometimes almost not going to the bathroom in time. I'm talking about coming downstairs and just about saying, 'Good morning'. [he mumbles] And seven hours later saying, 'Good night'. As you study the ocean – we lived on the ocean. That's all my wife got as communication for four years. I could not have the patience she had. My temperament, after about the third month, I would say 'JESUS CHRIST! SAY SOMETHING. HOW CAN YOU SIT THERE LIKE THAT! SHITTING ON YOURSELF!' [he shouts] Never. That's heroism, in my book.

Anyway. So you bounce around from one doctor to another, until you finally find the doctor who . . . part of my depression was a medical imbalance, and I have to take medicines the rest of my life. And the other was partly social. I had to stop drinking any kind of alcohol, because if you take alcohol and anti-depressants you will make the biggest hole you have ever had in your life. And I fought my way out of it, you know, with Paula's help. And that's my . . . I believe nature gives you a gift. And the bigger the gift, you'd better watch your bum because it's gonna come collect something later on. [audience laughs] I believe that. I believe

202

it, you know. Anyway. So that's the problem with the depression.

T.H.: What about the future, Rod? What about things like Beethoven, you mentioned? I mean, is there any possibility?

R.S.: No. I don't think that'll happen. Won't happen in films. May happen in television. But I don't think it'll happen in American television. No I don't . . . No. I don't think that'll happen. But that's all right. You gotta have a dream, you know. I respect the person who reaches for a star and misses it because they never slide back as far as where they began. You know what I mean? That's why in acting I go overboard sometimes, because I believe acting should be the highest form of joy or the highest form of pain, put in the theatrical fashion. I do believe the actor must entertain first. I mean Stanislavsky did his production when he wanted to be real and he had knights in armour – real armour, and real horses on the stage, and they pulled him up on cables on to the horse. And the critics said, 'Mr Stanislavsky, had we wanted a lecture on history we would have gone to college.' And they were right. There was no time to wait five minutes while they hoisted the sky up.

T.H.: One of the things I noticed when I watched *The Untouchables* again with Robert De Niro. His performance seemed very largely yours as Al Capone. Which of the young actors like De Niro do you respect. If any?

R.S.: Oh my God, yeah. One of the most brilliant performers I've ever seen is Daniel Day-Lewis. *My Left Foot.* Playing a person like that, whatever it is. If he makes one false move, it can be sickeningly comic. Know what I mean? Embarrassingly comical all of a sudden. Takes guts. That's what I mean. I go for actors who take a chance, like Jack Nicholson, when I saw the *Witches of Eastwick*, he did. In the last scene, most actors I know, they would have got a little upset. But they would have played it safe. But he goes for it. He took the scene and lifted it up forty feet. Nobody could do that. The director couldn't have done that. The cameraman couldn't do that. Only the actor can do that, you know. De Niro, Hoffman, you know, Daniel Day-Lewis, Pacino. What I feel now is – I may be wrong, I'm only speaking about my country, and that is . . . I don't hear any echoes of new names coming from a young position in the distance. I don't hear after De Niro, after Hoffman, Daniel Day-Lewis, though he's English.

T.H.: I know you have strong views about silence in movies . . .

R.S.: Well, strangely enough, I always thought what happened had started with the James Bond films. But it became malignant later on. By that I mean the James Bond films you kinda said, 'Oh well, it's tongue in cheek. They're blowing up', and what happened, it kept increasing and increasing until now the writer gets himself into a position that he can't write himself out of it, so the next thing you know the woman is blown up, the car goes over the cliff, the house explodes, and now in America, anyway, two things have taken over films, in my opinion.

Marketing. Number one. And Jack Nicholson is a clever son of a gun, let me tell you. He took a little money up front on *Batman* and took a percentage of the T-shirts, toys. He's gonna make forty or fifty million dollars. One picture. Now, I'm not knocking him. An actor should get everything. You get my point. Marketing has become more important. And the technical things have become more important. But part of that, underneath it, is also because as I said before, we want to see a little something different. Because we get reels of them all day on television. When we go to the movies, I think we want to see a little more circus. A little more exciting. Still with the realities, still with the truth, you know.

T.H.: What is the biggest risk you've taken as an actor?

R.S.: I got up this morning. [audience laughs] Well, the most difficult scene, one of the most difficult scenes I ever did, because it was me and the camera, was in *The Pawnbroker* when I put my hand down, and I kept saying, 'Jesus Christ. I hope the audience believes this is happening.' And a funny thing happened. I'll make a confession. It's terrible. I worked for days at home. That's another thing. I think the American actor should do more homework. Acting would go up sixty per cent more. Actors are sloppy. They come in half asleep. They got the coffee, the cigarette. I mean, when I see my daughter prepare for an opera or a ballet dancer doing their exercises I feel so ashamed. I feel so ashamed to walk in and say, 'What scene are we doing?' And they don't do their homework. Now what was the question? I forgot the question.

T.H.: The biggest risk.

R.S.: Well that was one of the toughest scenes I ever did.

T.H.: In *The Pawnbroker*.

R.S.: Yeah. But I wanted you to believe it, but Tom, what happened was I worked so hard at home to put that hand down, right? And I thought I had it, I thought I felt it. I remember my hand getting caught . . . we had a car once in America called the Packard. Which is a bit like a Rolls-Royce. Well, I got four of my fingers caught in the Packard door when I was a kid. Somebody slammed it, and to this day, I can't forget that feeling. So this is acting technique for some people. I started to remember the Packard, the colour of the Packard, where it took place, when I banged my hand . . . all these crazy things I do to . . . actors prepare in all different ways. And I thought I had it, so I came in, and I got there, and they say 'You're ready?' and I walk up and down. Jersey Joe Woolcott who was a fighter . . . I did a picture called *The Harder They Fall* – the last picture of Humphrey Bogart – he watched me one day and said, 'Jesus, man, you must have walked thirty miles,' he says, 'You do more road work than I do!' 'Cos I'm nervous I'll walk about till I'm ready. 'I'll be out there in a minute. Where am I? Oh yes . . . Are we starting here? Yes. OK.' Anyway, I got there. It was going well, and I got it down, and let me tell you what I forgot. What do you think I forgot? How to take it off. How to take the hand off. I got so worried I would convince you that I was putting the thing through my hand. I forgot I had to take it off. I never rehearsed that part! And the camera's turning. Now what saved me was panic again. I believe terror . . . the fear of failure has made my life a success. [audience laughs] It's true. In any profession. You swear to God you're not going to do it, I mean, that's another story. Anyway, I remembered when I was in pain I'd hold my breath. So what I did was I held my breath. I held my breath. Thank God it wasn't in colour. I would look like a tomato by the time we got to the end. And I went and let my hand go. I got away with it. But that was an acting challenge because there was no dialogue, there was no music, there was nothing that was used to spindle on that.

T.H.: One personal question, Rod, I've always wanted to know. Who did you base the movie tycoon on in *The Big Knife*?

R.S.: Oh. Nobody really, what happened was Clifford Odets the American playwright wrote that, and I came to Hollywood and everybody thought I was doing Harry Cohn, and Louis B. Mayer, and they . . . Louis B. Mayer mostly. And he was dead long before I got to Hollywood. And people would say, 'You did Louis B. Mayer. You did Louis B. Mayer,' and I would say, 'I don't think I did Louis B. Mayer, he was dead you know.' That's another thing, when I did *Waterloo* and played Napoleon. I had two men in this city telling me they had tea with him every Wednesday. [audience laughs] That's a true story. And let me tell you, I stood there like that and said, 'I'm sure you did, sir.' [more laughs] 'Can I stir it for you? Would you like a little more sugar?' [more laughs]

T.H.: Rod, we're nearly at the end of our conversation. And I know a lot of people would like to ask questions – well I hope a lot of people would like to ask questions. So anybody who would like to ask a question, which is known as throwing it open to the audience.

R.S.: Don't all scream at once.

Q: Would you tell us something about *The Loved One*?

R.S.: *The Loved One*, yeah. I got the part of Joyboy, and he was a man who made his living painting corpses so they should look good when relatives come to see them. And one of the memories of my life I will never forget is me painting the dead face of Sir John Gielgud. [audience laughs] He was playing one of the corpses, right? And there's things that happen in acting. All of a sudden you have to be careful you don't get out of yourself. I'm doing my part and I'm painting the face, and a voice says to me, 'This is John Gielgud. This is Sir John Gielgud. You're painting his face. Don't paint him too hard.' [audience laughs] What happened, now this guy . . . that's a good question. An actor . . . I'll tell you another story, if we've got another hour and a half. [audience laughs]

Right. I didn't know what to do about the part and Tony
Richardson said, 'Oh, Rod, would you come in, we'd like to
talk. It would be super. Oh super. Super. Oh so super.' [feigns
English accent] And he was a wonderful director and a
wonderful man, and a man that took chances on the set. And
they were shooting at a big Hollywood estate with all these
crazy statues around. And I got out of the car and I was
walking up to go where they were shooting, and there was
this bust. A Bacchus. A Dionysius with curly hair in white
concrete. I said, 'Jesus God. There's my part. There's my part,'
and Tony . . . I said, 'How are you? We don't talk about
anything. Come here I want to show you something.' I said,
'There it is. That strawberry look. I want the silver curly hair.
I want the white powder on the face. The man is not
homosexual. He's not male. He's neuter gender. He's a
eunuch.' I said, 'This is it. A Bacchus,' and he said, 'Super.
Simply super. Yes.' [in English accent – audience laughs]
Yeah, but you see with him you could have fun.

Now I'll tell you about the joys of acting. In many scripts it
says, 'He answers the phone'. And I'm the crazy type. Tony
and I now, we trusted each other, 'cos we showed each other
what we could do and that's why you're left alone. You
earned each other's respect. And I said, 'Tony. There must be
another way to answer a phone,' and he says . . . he knew
the light, and when the director knows and he sees the light
in my eyes – 'Don't you start!' [audience laughs] 'Don't you
start.' I said, 'I'll tell you what. Have a shot of the telephone
here.' And this guy had barbells in his room, right? This is the
screen. You see the phone here. There's the edge of the bed
here. The phone rings – BRRRING – Nobody answers –
BRRRING – and you see him, with the weight, come back off
the bed. Then go back down out of the picture – BRRRING –
Go back down. Finally drops away. Upside down and answers
the phone and says 'Hello'. That's one of the joys of acting.
Isn't it? That's why we improvise like that.

T.H.: Another question.

Q: What role has given you the greatest satisfaction?

R.S.: I think my best work is in *The Pawnbroker*. The last scene, where I find the boy dead on the street. I think that's the highest moment, whatever it may be, with my talent, whatever it may be. I'll tell you again. This is very interesting. An actor must know a little bit about everything, and only be a master of acting if he's lucky. By that I . . . Well, I'll tell you a story. It wasn't too difficult, as you can see, for me to get emotional, right? There was the dead boy in the street. OK, that's my beloved . . . That's my daughter Anna. [crying] Dead. So I had that. And I'm waiting. And they say 'ACTION' and I come in and I kneel down. And this was done right outside with four hundred people watching all around. And I put my hand in the chocolate syrup. 'Cos they didn't have blood then. It was black and white. But because I'm an actor and that is my daughter it becomes blood to me. Then I really started to go to pieces. And it said in the script he puts his head back, and he screams. I started to put my head back and open my mouth to scream, and in that one millionth of a second, my mind became Picasso's painting of *Guernica* – the destruction of the town of Guernica. Right? This is happening in a millionth, in a millionth, in a millionth of a . . . no computer goes as fast as your brain . . . of a second. My intellect said, 'Jesus, that's good.' My instincts were right. It was my daughter. And my creative ability said, 'Don't make a sound.' [utters slowly] Because when I saw the painting of Picasso those figures he had with the painted tongues were some of the loudest screams I ever heard in my life and obviously a painting can't scream. And that moment to me, was a moment I'll never forget. Don't ask me why.

Now, just to clarify what I'm talking about, I don't like to teach acting because it's exhausting. A friend of mine . . . a

209

friend of mine . . . a man who was my first teacher had to pay the rent, he couldn't pay the rent. He said, 'Rod, would you' . . . his wife called up, 'He's sick. Please could you take over his acting class.' I'm shooting in the daytime *Al Capone* and kind of directing. I said yes because of my respect for him. He was a little man from the Moscow Arts Theatre. A very good teacher. He taught me two things. He taught me respect . . . and enthusiasm. He wasn't that good an acting teacher but, Jesus, he was good for those two things, and it was a good thing I met him in the very beginning. So I came in and I conducted my class. I sat down, and over here were two reproduction Van Gogh paintings, a reproduction of Cézanne, a reproduction of Rembrandt. Over here was a victrola where I played *Claire de Lune* by Debussy, Beethoven's. I recited a poem by e.e. cummings, Robert Frost, a passage from Shakespeare. I read from *Life* Magazine, the Olympics were going on and how different performers in races got themselves ready. One man stayed up all night and because he was so afraid he wouldn't be able to win the race, he won. Others waited for the . . . [audience laughs] no, this is all preparation. How different people prepare. That he won the race, and then I told a couple of jokes. It took about two hours and a half, and then I shut the books and I said, 'Now, if none of this touches you, get your ass out of this profession. Because an actor has to know a little bit about painting, a little bit about music. You're working and the director says to you, '"Well this is the kind of guy that would spit on a Van Gogh. I know. Oh I got him. Oh I know that son of a bitch. Oh yes."'

Then for *The Pawnbroker*. I got the part in *The Pawnbroker* by going to the dentist. I went to the dentist and I'm sitting there, and there were *Life* Magazines. And I go through them and, Jesus Christ, a special issue on Treblinka, Dachau, Auschwitz. You know the gods are kind. The pawnbroker's problem was he sentenced himself as guilty for not rescuing his family from the concentration camps. And everyone with a rational mind would say to him – see I make up stories outside of the thing – 'Ten million soldiers couldn't have rescued them. Don't be like that.' And then what does he do, because he's not that sick to kill himself, he exists in society . . . but if you notice in the first part of the picture, he hardly looks anyone in the eye. And the only time he looks anybody straight in the eye is when a man sees the tattooed numbers of the concentration camp and says, 'What's the numbers for?' My favourite line in the picture, he says, 'That's for walking on water,' and the rest of the line in modern day would be, 'You jackass'. You know. But that's why an actor has to be . . . has to be alive, and know a little bit about . . . you never know. You never know what your stimulation is going to come from. What's going to get your curiosity going. What's going to turn your imagination on. Personal things. Sounds. Smells. I don't know.

T.H.: Tell us about in *No Way to Treat a Lady*. The camp hairdresser.

R.S.: Oh. I like *No Way to Treat a Lady* 'cos I said to myself, if Peter Sellers can play a lot of parts, I want a chance to play a lot of parts. That's not true really but I thought about that later. [audience laughs] Anyway. I'll have a drink on that. Anyway. This is what actors go through, and at those prices believe me I'm not complaining. It's a hundred and twenty-three degrees on the set in an old brownstone building in New York. It is ten minutes after six and we are shooting. We are supposed to stop at six. But when a scene is going, if you are any kind of an actor you don't stop. It's like a telephone in the middle . . . an idiot answers a telephone when he's making love, because it destroys everything. 'Hello, how are you? I'll be right with you, darling.' [audience laughs] I mean the whole thing, the spontaneity is gone. And there's two actresses in the scene I'm playing with, and they know I like to improvise, and I was playing this kind of gay person, and all of a sudden one of them, which was not in the script, said, 'You better get outta here, you homo,' and I said, 'Well, [puts on a strange voice] what are you talking about. It takes one to know one?' And the director said, 'Great. We'll shoot that rap,' and I said, 'No way. That's one of the biggest Goddamn clichés I ever heard, "It takes one to know one".' Now my make-up was running. Jack Smight the director, a lovely man, knew me like a brother. I said, 'Jack. I can't, I don't want to do any more. We're supposed to leave at six. It's a quarter after six. I know you can't have the actresses tomorrow, they have cost you money, but we won't need them. All you do is call me homo off-stage when I go to the door in a three-quarter shot and grab the knob of the door. You say the word off-stage and I'll come around with something.' But he trusted me. I mean directors have gone crazy, but I said, 'I don't know. I'll come around with something.' A twenty million dollar picture and I say 'I'll come around with something.' [audience laughs]

Anyway, I go home and I go out that night to a little actor's bar which became very famous. Now you have it over here, it's called Joe Allen's, and there's this gay guy, and he and I always used to banter with each other. And I said, 'How are you tonight, sweetheart?' and he said, 'I'm all right. How are you?' I said, 'Boy. You've got your own squadron, right? You haven't touched ground in years.' He said, 'Listen. It doesn't mean that you're a bad person.' I said, 'What kind of wine do you like?' He got very serious. He said, 'What do you mean, Rod?' I said, 'Name me the kind of wine you like. If you could have. What would you have?' He said, 'La Tache.' I said, 'You just got a case.' Now I went home. Now Jack sees me come in. He sees my lines. AHA! [audience laughs] The kid is up to something. Right? He says 'What's the lines?' 'I'm not going to tell you.' [audience laughs] He says, 'Come on.' I said, 'I'm not going to tell you.' So it is. OK, I went to the door. I hit the door knob. It started to turn. He said, 'Homo.' I said, 'Doesn't mean you're a bad person.' We pulled three takes. Three times we tried to shoot it and three times we broke ourselves up. And that again shows you what goes into acting and where it can come from.

T.H.: Another question, please.

Q: Have you turned anything down, which in retrospect you wish you hadn't?

R.S.: *Patton*. Oh yeah. *Patton*. Yeah.

T.H.: Was that the only thing?

R.S.: Outside of my bed. [audience laughs] Yeah I think so. Yeah. I think that's the worst mistake I made from a business point of view. But as I said before, when you're healthy and you've just got the Academy award, you're cocky and you think you're on top of the world. The stronger your mind . . . your health is, the stronger your mind is the stronger your philosophy is, and when you're tired and weak, as I said before, I would have crawled on my knees if I needed the money to play *Patton*. You know. I've done things I didn't want to do. Now you wanna talk about another side about acting. We have a human being called an actor who's in a depression. We have a business manager who calls up. He's been a friend of this business manager for some twenty-seven odd years. Called his agent unbeknown to the actor, 'cos he doesn't want to upset him, and he said, 'Listen. Rod's getting to the point where he's going to have to sell some of his assets. We gotta get him a job someplace.' Now the town must have known I was sick 'cos there were no offers. So I got a job . . . Stirling Silliphant who wrote *In the Heat of the*

213

Night wrote a terrible script. And his wife was in the lead.
And I wound up in Argentina. I didn't take that job. I took
the job for the money. I know I needed it. But I took that job
to see if I could walk. Talk. And remember. To hell with the
performance. The thing of this human being called actor is
trying to find out if you can function on any level. And
you're in a bowl of jelly walking around, in ice-cold, greasy
jelly, all around you. You know. And I do not apologize.
Because had I not done that kind of crap to see if I could still
cope . . . you see there was no creativity. Because I came to
the set wrapped in the terror of the fear of failure, and I . . .
you know . . . I don't remember like I told you about the
theatre. I, to this day . . . you know, one day I said to Brian, 'I
don't know what happens to me, Jesus Christ.' I said the
other day, 'I always think I won't remember. I won't be able
to do it. I won't remember.' And he said, 'You haven't
changed since nineteen fifty.' [audience laughs] I said,
'Was I like that in nineteen fifty?' He said, 'The same
conversation.'

So . . . it's my responsibility as a hunter. I believe men are
hunters in our society, in the sense, instead of skin we now
go out and get dollar bills and bring them home. It's my
responsibility to come back to my cave, where my wife is,
with something to put the bread on the table, and I'm not
excusing myself. But I did that for two reasons. One to see if I
was still alive and could feel anything – just the pressure of
the carpet on the sole of my foot. And, two, to get some
money before I had to sell anything. Maybe a painting that I
loved or something like that.

Q: When your story was told by David Chapman in one of
your international years, he says that your precursor in
Hollywood was Charles Laughton. I would like to ask you
how you feel about this comparison, and of the older stars
who you saw as a youngish person in older films. Who were

your ideals and great impressions which you had among the older ones?

R.S.: Who impressed me the most? That was the question?

T.H.: That's right. You have been compared with Charles Laughton as a precursor.

R.S.: That's flattery. Laughton was probably one of the most imaginative actors that ever was filmed. A lot of actors aren't very imaginative. I mean, Laughton could eat a breakfast, and you would say, 'Well that's the way you eat a breakfast.' Right? And it was his way.

Paul Muni was my idol because I believe actors are supposed to create different human beings. When I hear an actor of today say, 'Well I don't know if I can do that. I don't think I can play that. That's bad for my image,' I say, 'You poor son of a bitch. You only got one image?' You're supposed to create a lot of people. Paul Muni, Charles Laughton. Those people I admired a great deal. A great deal. My favourite actor that impressed me was a French actor. An incredible talent named Harry Baur. And I remember when I saw him . . . In New York in the summer time they have a little theatre called the Failure Theatre and they play all the European films. And all the actors would go there. You could tell because their eyes were red. They looked like bull's eyes when they were at the end of the summer. Like that, you know. In one day they'd do *Grande Illusion* and *Carnet de Bal*. The next day they'd do Beethoven and *The Importance of Being Earnest*. And Harry Baur, when he did *Les Miserables*, and played both parts . . . That I would love to have . . . This man had the ability to stand still, and he'd made a universe around himself. Incredible. And James Cagney's energy. Jesus Christ, where did that man get his energy? [audience laughs] He makes me tired when I see him in pictures, you know.

215

[audience laughs] I met him. He was a nice man. He wrote a lot of poetry. He read me some of his poetry.

T.H.: What about that risk-taking in *White Heat* when he goes mad?

R.S.: Yeah. Hello, Mom! I'm on top of the world! Look at me, Mom!

T.H.: So, another question, please.

Q: A little bit more about *Al Capone*.

R.S.: I knew you'd say that. [audience laughs] When you were walking down the aisle I said, 'You see that man in the ... That man's going to ask me about Al Capone.' Al Capone. I'll tell you a story about Al Capone. They first come to me with the script. And I'm on my semi-idealistic high horse, even though nobody knew me much in Hollywood then. And I said, 'I'm not doing a gangster.' So they come back, after, with their great wisdom, and their original way of attacking you ... with more money. [audience laughs] They haven't got the brains to approach you any other way, right? 'Well, we'll give you one half more.' I said, 'I don't want any...' [ends in a mumble, audience laughs] They tripled it. And there was more money at that time than I had ever ... I said, 'I don't wanna ...' He said, 'What do you want to do?' I said, 'I don't like the script.' And the guy said, 'Well if you don't like the goddamn script why don't you re-write it.' I said, 'Gimme the goddamn script.' And I went home and for a month I re-wrote it and I brought him in a cast list. Martin Balsam, Nicky Persoff. People they hadn't seen I got from the Actors' Studio. And I said, 'And I still won't do it unless I get ten days rehearsal.'
   Now in nineteen fifty-seven, to utter the word rehearsal in

Hollywood, they committed you to the insane asylum. [audience laughs] Immediately you were taken and gone. I figured, 'Fine. That's it. I'm outta here. Fine.' Five days go by, and this is how my mind works. They say, 'OK Rod, we'll give you seven days rehearsal.' Unheard of. And this is how I live I guess. I said, 'You son of a bitch. We're playing poker. You call me. You call me. OK. One man to another. Yeah. I'll go with seven days rehearsal. Let's see what happens.' And we did it. Now the big problem with *Al Capone* for me again was why? Why does Al Capone tell the woman he loves, whose husband he killed, that he killed him? I mean do you want to get rid of a lover fast? 'Hi there, darling, I killed your husband.' [audience laughs] I said he was too smart for that. It had to come out of a character weakness, if you know what I'm talking about. I said, 'OK. Give me a tape recorder,' and they gave me a tape recorder and I went in the room with Fay Spain A lovely woman who is no longer with us. A lovely actress. I said, 'Faye. Do me a . . . Just keep asking me, "Did you kill my husband?"' And we were in that room for about an hour and a half, I came up with more answers you couldn't see. And I said, 'Don't be ridiculous.' She said finally, 'You killed my husband?' and I said, 'YES!!' [he shouts] His temper, right? Character weakness. The yes came out, before he had a chance to stop it. I could believe that. That's human behaviour. I could accept that. I could play the scene.

Now we get ready to shoot, and this is the thing that scared me to death. Phone rings. Voice from Chicago says, 'I represent a group of people,' [puts on gangster voice – audience laughs] 'and they'd like to see the script,' [audience laughs] 'and they'd like to see a picture of the actor who's going to play the part.' And by now we're scraping . . . we're talking. He said, 'I am a lawyer who represents a group of people.' We're talking to the Mafia. The whole audience knows. Everybody in the office knew we were talking to people who put concrete on your face, right? [audience

laughs] A script was sent 'toutie-suitie'. [audience laughs]
Now what happens is, three days later everybody says, 'I
represent a group of people in Chicago. You can do the
picture.' And don't think they couldn't stop it if they didn't
want to. A few broken legs here and there. And I said, 'Why
did they want a picture of the actor? For Christ's sakes!'
[audience laughs] 'Cos they wanted to make sure he didn't
look like a pansy. [audience laughs] It's a true story.

Now the picture's over. And it's been released. And I'm
invited by Budd Schulberg, the man who wrote *On the
Waterfront*, to go to a party. And I go to this party. And there's
a man with silver, beautiful hair. A bluish-grey single-breasted
suit. Another shade of blue shirt. With like a silver-blue tie.
And he looked like . . . anyway, he was gorgeous. Six foot
two, and he came over and said, 'Mr Steiger. My name is
Johnny D. I would just like to say we're very happy with
what you did for Mr Capone.' And I said, 'Thank you, sir.'
And he walked away. And I said to Budd, 'God! Who is that?'
He says, 'Johnny D. Number three in the mob.' [audience
laughs] 'Wait a minute! Supposing he'd said he didn't like it!'
[he shouts – audience laughs] 'Holy Jesus, I would have been
tipped.' That's a true story. And every person I met from the
underworld said, and the man had been dead more than
twenty years, 'Mr Capone'. Very interesting. Mr Capone. 'We
liked what you did for Mr Capone.'

Q: What was it like working with Humphrey Bogart?

R.S.: The man was one of the nicest people I ever met. He
and I got along. He accepted me and I was so pleased, and I
have great respect for him. Because he was a survivor and he
was a very good actor. He also . . . His strongest quality was in
that of being a creative actor, more or less like Charles
Laughton, but he had a great authority. Because he would be
doing a scene, and he'd say, 'I don't like the ketchup on the

spring burger of a broccoli, and anyway you gotta get out of here.' And you accepted it, and about ten seconds later you'd say, 'The burger on the springboard with the broccoli? What the hell was he talking about?' [audience laughs] And for that moment you say, 'Oh yeah. I don't like burger with the spring . . .' [audience laughs] 'I don't like it. I hate it.'

So we did jokes on each other. I found out one day – the whole New York gang used to hang out in the dressing room on the set – and they said, 'He's got one of these newspapers where you make your own headlines.' Right? 'And he says he's going to give it to you. He's going to come in and hand it to you.' So I go out and I had one made out. And I put it in my sleeve. And he comes in. 'How you doing, Rod?' Right? [audience laughs] And I said, 'I'm doing all right.' He says, 'I got something for you.' And as he pulls his out I pull mine out at the same time. [audience laughs] His says, 'Brando in town. Steiger leaves.' [audience laughs] Mine said, 'Bogart begs for acting classes from Steiger.' [audience laughs and applauds]

Now, one day I'm coming to work and he's not on the schedule. He's not supposed to work that day. I said, 'B . . .' I never called him Bogey. I called him Mr Bogart, again 'cos I think . . . Anyway I said, 'What you doing for Christ's sake. Get some rest. It's your day off.' And he had to do some close-ups. He said, 'My eyes are watering.' And I said, 'Oh. Oh, OK.' Then, life went on. Two weeks later somebody said, 'Mr Bogart died today,' and this voice in my ears said, 'My eyes are watery.' Jackass, and I was . . . the man was in pain, wasn't he? Sure. That's why his eyes watered. Shows you how we miss things sometimes. I was so busy with my . . . and he never said a word. He died. That was his last picture. He was dying of cancer at the time. He never complained of it. I'll never forget that voice in my ears. And he was a wonderful man. He was a wonderful, wonderful man to work with. I liked him.

Q: Do you have fond memories of *The Mark*?

R.S.: Yes. I have fond memories of *The Mark*. I want to do it again. And I can't get the rights to it because child abuse in America now is a big thing. And the picture – don't know if you ever saw *The Mark* – The picture is about a man who's got a problem. He's attracted to young children. And he finally picks one out of a playground and he takes the child away to molest her. And he stops himself. He's repugnant. All of a sudden he can't do it. He's not that sick really. He throws up and he comes to the police station with the child, and says, 'This is the child I was going to do this and this and that.' Right? And they persecuted him as if he had done it. And that's why I did the picture. 'Cos I often wonder, people who are accused of crimes they didn't really do and how their lives are destroyed.

See, they put him in prison. He gets an analyst in prison. He gets out of prison. But everywhere . . . He gets a job in an office. I remember that wonderful actor Donald Wolfit had the scene with him where he says, 'Well, it's a bit embarrassing. Evidently you had a problem in the past.' And then the scene that killed me. He falls in love with Maria Schell who has this six-year-old child. And he's coming to have dinner at her house with them, and she knows now. But he doesn't know that she knows. And he comes through the door, and her six-year-old goes to run towards him and jump in his arms and she says, 'NO!' And everything stops. Then they do a close-up of the boy, him, the girl, him, the wife and he turns around and walks out. You know. Broke your . . . and now I would like . . . I played the psychiatrist in it. I played the psychiatrist, and now I'm too old, but I could play the psychiatrist now. I would love to do that again in America because it's very . . .

T.H.: Who would play the man?

R.S.: I would hope an actor like Daniel Day-Lewis. Any real good, fine actor. The best actor that they could get. And I gotta tell you that a compliment . . . far be it for me to brag about myself but, if you got another hour. [audience laughs] I was invited by the American Psychiatric Association to go to their convention and do a lecture on being a psychiatrist. [audience laughs] And I said, 'What am I gonna do?' In the first place, this is again why. And they said, 'OK. You got me, and this is so, and you've got a few dollars at the box office and were going to shoot this.' And I said to the director, 'Well, just a second. In the script it says he is a . . . in the social system. In the social civil service in this particular . . . of England.' And then he says, 'Yes.' And then I said, 'Well then I can't have an American accent. I don't believe it.' He said, 'Well, we have some . . .' And I said, 'But we don't have enough problems.' And because I was mad at the producer, the producer said, 'Well, what accent are you going to use?' and without thinking I said, 'I'm going to use a pidgin Irish.' And his face went white. Who ever heard of an Irish psychiatrist, right? [audience laughs] And I played him Irish. I had a great time. Not only that. I made sure . . . I had gone to a doctor who needed a shave. He had too many patients. He was a chainsmoker. I also put in he was a coffee drinker. I was going crazy, and then the thing that I put in that I loved most. He is dealing with this patient – trying to help him. The phone rings. He picks it up and he says, 'What? Helen, I told you. Don't call me at the office!' [audience laughs] And you knew that he had problems in his life.

Q: Were you responsible for choosing tonight's screening of *The Pawnbroker*, and what was it like playing a film of such bleakness for you, such an emotional man?

R.S.: What was the first part of the question?

T.H.: Were you responsible for choosing *The Pawnbroker* tonight? In fact he wasn't. I was. [audience laugh]
  But what was it like playing a film of such bleakness?

R.S.: Well, I don't believe that an actor who says, 'I'm doing this part,' will live it day and night. This is a bad thing to do. Because your mind has to get away from it to rest correctly. And secondly, if it rests correctly, it means your imagination gets refurbished and can help you do your next day's work. But when you're playing a heavy part like that, there's a lot less laughter in the house of Steiger, right? [audience laughs] I mean, you kinda come home. You're polite or you're just quiet. You kinda say this is calm or this is nice or wonderful, and of course, you gotta go to bed, you know. I gotta go to bed. And you check over your work for the next day. Now when I'm home and on the set I maintain that atmosphere. I talked to no one hardly in *The Pawnbroker*. They thought I was, I don't know, egotistical crap all the time. But I didn't because I was trying to keep myself in some kind of calm, and sadness. Now, when I did *No Way to Treat a Lady* they couldn't shut me up! [audience laughs] You know, I was coming in telling jokes because I wanted to have the atmosphere. And let me tell you something else. An actor always has an audience. When you work in movies you got sixty people watching you. That's like a real theatre as far as I'm concerned. If I were in the studio and there was a camera that worked automatically, and there was a camera in me and there was a cat in the corner, you can bet your little bum that when the scene is over I look to see if I got the cat's attention. [audience laughs] And when I work, I don't care so much about the director. I mean I respect them. I see if the crew and the grips have put down their racing form. [audience laughs]
  Oh yes! If you get some of these old timers who've seen Bogart and Rooney and they've been doing this for forty-two

years. Putting the furniture in and painting the set. You don't care if his name is whatever it is, you know. All of a sudden when you see two out of five of them looking at you. Or the highest compliment when you somehow touched their humanity. There's strange things they do. They pick up the paper to leave the set and they kind of go . . . [makes a noise – audience laughs] Or they give you a wink, you know.

T.H.: When's that happened? Or what movie is that? Can you remember?

R.S.: I did the speech about the Jews. I did a speech about the Jewish people, and you could pick out every Jew in Manhattan for forty miles around. Boy. You know. The faces, white like that, and they came over. Now I gotta tell you. This is a confession. Right? This is the second act. Are you ready? Anyway. [interviewer laughs] I did a picture called *The Chosen*. I don't know if any of you ever saw it, where I play a rabbi. First night's shooting I'm overwhelmed because they're shooting at a location in Brooklyn Heights and my house is a half a block around the corner. Which means I go home for my supper. I mean I've got it made. I walk a half a block. I do my movie. I couldn't believe it. So I'm sitting there and I've studied. I've snuck into the Hassidic group in New York. They're not allowed in. They're not allowed to go to movies. I sneak in. I watch things. I study. I'm sitting there now, and I've got the beard I've grown for two months. I've got that big, wide fur hat. I've got the satin coats on and everything, and I'm sitting there. And I feel pretty good. I never . . . you know . . . I didn't think I feel . . . you know, I just feel comfortable. This is the first night, and the first night is like the first night with the first date. You're a nervous wreck, right? And the assistant director says, 'Rod.' I say, 'Yeah!' Right? He says, 'We're going to do the dance.' [audience laughs] I don't read directions when I read a script. And when I read over that description I thought there was going to be a dance at the wedding. And the head rabbi has to lead the dance! [audience laughs] And there's everybody there getting ready. The dance. The wedding. Things costing thousands of dollars. The camera. The extras. I'm running around, and a couple of rabbis say, 'Make a gesture for Christ's sakes!' [audience laughs] Tell me. What should I do? What should I do? What should I do? And they gave me a couple of things. And I don't know how to phrase this. I did a crazy thing. I wanted to get a certain . . . a certain feeling. And I pretended I was doing a dance of love to God. So he should forgive me my sins. Don't ask me where I got it from. That's what makes one actor different to the other. Justification. Justification of what you're supposed to do. That's why one actor says hello and you never forget it. And another actor says hello and you couldn't . . . there's nothing to remember. It didn't come from him.

Shirley Booth, one of our best actresses. She had a scene. And she has to come in and load groceries in *Come Back, Little Sheba*. And she comes in and she was wonderful. Natural actressing. She unloaded the groceries, except it took about three hundred and forty-two hours! [audience laughs] And we're in the theatre. And theatre time is not real time. And Danny Mann the director said, 'Shirley. I don't know what to say,' 'cos she's one of the great actresses. He was embarrassed. He didn't know what to say. He said, 'Shirley. It's gotta be faster.' [audience laughs] She says, 'All right.' She was a little bitty woman. She says, 'All right.' She put the groceries out. She came back and she did the same thing! The same movement! Without looking like she was going faster, but it was faster. And Danny Mann said, 'God bless you, Shirley. How did you do it?' She said, 'There's a taxi outside with the meter running.' [audience laughs]

So, that's it. Imagination nobody can give you. The quality of it nobody can guarantee you, you know.

T.H.: Any more questions, please?

R.S.: I'm getting warmed up.

Q: Have you ever considered writing your memoirs?

R.S.: No. After the Marquis De Sade. No. [audience laughs] No. I . . . people have asked me that. See, I'm just a frustrated poet. I've been writing poetry since I was . . . well I call it poetry . . . and, I went to New York. I wanted to publish my poems in a little book, paperback. Somebody said to me once, 'What would you like?' I said, 'I'd like to have one poem that people repeat a line of after I'm dead. Miles to go before I sleep, Miles to go . . . one, oh my God . . . you know.' And of course they said, 'The poems are nice. Now what about a book of your life? We'll do the poems later.' Well you know they're not going to do the poems later because they have the book of your life, right? And I don't think my life . . . There's so many things going on. So many people have such tragedy and stuff. I feel embarrassed. My life is a nice kind of drama, but nothing compared to people starving in it, the wars and . . . you know. But what I wanted to do . . . I said, 'OK. I'll write a book about each picture I did,' like I'm talking to you here tonight. And I'd like to do a one man show like this in London, by the way – which is what I'm auditioning for tonight. [audience laughs – and applauds] So what happened was that I would put one of my poems at the beginning of each chapter. And I thought, never mind the value of my poems as literature. But the closest you'll ever get to me's gotta be in my poems. And if you don't know what I'm like by chapter seven, you ain't never gonna know what I'm like. 'Cos when I'm sorry for myself or whatever, things I believe in – like when I was seventeen I wrote a poem *I Am* . . . This was about the sexes. Men and women. 'I love you like you are of me. Yet being so much as one, we are different. That difference contains a need. And that need desired and pursued, with respect, makes us both more completely ourselves.' You know. That's my stuff. And that's what I wanted to sneak in. When you read that you say, 'This guy. He thinks a little. He thinks a little maybe.' So that's how I wanted to sneak it in. Did I answer the question?

T.H.: You answered the question.

Q: Professional conductor thanking you for *Al Capone* and saying he hopes you will do a Beethoven movie.

R.S.: Thank you very much. At least there's two of us. [audience laughs] At least there's two for us. I know it's getting late. I'll shut up if you want to go home.

T.H.: I think, in fact, it is time to wind up. And I'd like to thank you . . .

R.S.: No wait a minute, before you thank there's something I have to say . . . I have to say . . . out of my way . . . get back . . . [audience laughs] There's two goldfish in a bowl. [audience laughs] And there's a window, and the wind is coming through and the curtains are wafting with the breeze. And as we go in closer on the goldfish bowl, we see it's shivering. And we see one goldfish's bubbles coming out. Mouth faster. The other one starts to go faster. All of a sudden one goldfish hits the other goldfish. The other one hits him back with his fin. They go around the little castle and the coral patterned pebbles. And as he goes around the water begins to go from blue to peculiar, sickening purple. And you see little bits of gold flakes from the bodies of these fish. And in the middle of this microcosm out of the very centre, finally one goldfish stands up, with an eye hanging out, and a broken fish, and says 'All right! But if there's no God, who

226

changes the water?!!!' [He shouts. Audience laughs and applauds] Good night.

T.H.: Thank you very much indeed, ladies and gentlemen. We'll leave you with a clip from *Zhivago*. A very rarely seen extract which I happen to think is one of Rod's finest speeches.

R.S.: And Simon Callow cut my scene. Thank you very much.

Filmography

1. Teresa (1951)
2. On the Waterfront (1954) [Charlie Malloy].
3. Oklahoma! (1955) [Jud Fry]
4. Jubal (1955) [Pinky]
5. Court-Martial of Billy Mitchell, The (1955) [Major Allan Guillon]
6. Big Knife, The (1955) [Stanley Hoff]
7. Harder They Fall, The (1956) [Nick Benko]
8. Back from Eternity (1956)
9. Unholy Wife, The (1957)
10. Run of the Arrow (1957) aka Hot Lead (1957) [O'Meara]
11. Across the Bridge (1957) [Carl Schaffner]
12. Cry Terror! (1958) [Paul Hoplin]
13. Al Capone (1959) [Al Capone]
14. Seven Thieves (1960) [Paul Mason]
15. An einem Freitag um halb zwelf (1960)
16. On Friday at Eleven (1961) [Morgan]
17. Mark, The (1961) [Doctor Edmund McNally]
18. Longest Day, The (1962) [Destroyer Commander]
19. Convicts Four (1962) aka Reprieve
20. 13, West Street (1962) [Detective Sergeant Koleski]
21. Mani Sulla Città, Le (1963) aka Hands Over the City [Nottola]
22. Time of Indifference (1964) aka Gli Indifferenti

23. Pawnbroker, The (1965) [Sol Nazerman]
24. Man Named John (1965) aka E Venne un Uomo [Commentator]
25. Loved One, The (1965) [Mr Joyboy]
26. Doctor Zhivago (1965) [Komarovsky]
27. Ragazza e il Generale, La (1967) aka Girl and the General, The [The General]
28. Movie Maker, The (1967)
29. In the Heat of the Night (1967) [Bill Gillespie]
30. Sergeant, The (1968) [Master Sergeant Albert Callan]
31. No Way to Treat a Lady (1968) [Christopher Gill]
32. Three Into Two Won't Go (1969)
33. Illustrated Man, The (1969) [Carl]
34. Waterloo (1971) [Napoleon]
35. Happy Birthday, Wanda Jane (1971) [Juan Miranda]
36. Giù la Testa (1971) aka Duck, You Sucker (1971) aka Fistful of Dynamite, A (1971)
37. Heroes, The (1972)
38. Lolly-Madonna XXX (1973) aka Lolly-Madonna War, The (1973) [Laban Feather]
39. Mussolini: Ultimo Atto (1974) aka Last Days of Mussolini, The [Mussolini]
40. Lucky Luciano (1974) [Gene Giannini]
41. Innocents aux Mains Sales, Les (1975) aka Dirty Hands (1975) [Louis Wormser]
42. Hennessy (1975) [Niall Hennessy]
43. W.C. Fields and Me (1976) [W.C. Fields]
44. Portrait of a Hitman (1977) aka Jim Buck [Max Andreotti]
45. Jesus of Nazareth (1977) (TV mini-series) [Pontius Pilate]
45. Wolf Lake (1978) aka Honor Guard, The [Charlie]
46. F.I.S.T. (1978) [Senator Andrew Madison]
47. Breakthrough (1978) aka Sergeant Steiner (1978) [General Webster]
48. Love and Bullets (1979) [Joe Bomposa]

49. Amityville Horror, The (1979) [Father Delaney]
50. Lucky Star, The (1980) [Colonel Gluck]
51. Lion of the Desert (1980) [Mussolini]
52. Klondike Fever (1980) aka Jack London's Klondike Fever
53. Chosen, The (1981) [Red Saunders]
54. Cattle Annie and Little Britches (1982) [Tilghman]
55. Zauberberg, Der (1982) aka Magic Mountain, The (1982)
56. Cook & Peary: The Race to the Pole (1983) (TV) [Robert E. Peary]
57. Naked Face, The (1984) [Lt. McGreavy]
58. Glory Boys, The (1984) [Sokarev]
59. Hollywood Wives (1985) (TV mini-series) 1985 [Oliver Easterne]
60. Sword of Gideon (1986) (TV mini-series) aka Vengeance [Mordechai Samuels]
61. Last Contract, The (1986)
62. Kindred, The (1986) [Doctor Phillip Lloyd]
63. Catch the Heat (1987)
64. Desperado: Avalanche at Devil's Ridge (1988) (TV) [Silas Slaten]
65. American Gothic (1988)
66. Tennessee Nights (1989) [Judge Prescott]
67. Passion and Paradise (1989) (TV) [Sir Harry Oakes]
68. January Man (1989) [Eamon Flynn]
69. Men of Respect (1991) [Charlie D'Amico]
70. In the Line of Duty: Manhunt in the Dakotas (1991) (TV) aka Midnight Murders [Gordon Kahl]
71. Guilty as Charged (1991) [Ben Kallin]
72. Ballad of the Sad Café, The (1991) [Rev. Willin]
73. Sinatra (1992) (TV) [Sam Giancana]
74. Player, The (1992) [Himself]
75. Lincoln (1992) (TV) [Voice of Ulysses S. Grant]
76. Neighbour, The (1993) [Myron]
77. Earth and the American Dream (1993) [Voice-over]

78. Tales of the City (1993) (TV) aka Armistead Maupin's Tales of the City [Bookstore Owner]
79. Specialist, The (1994) [Joe Leon]
80. Seven Sundays (1994) [Benjamin]
81. Last Tattoo, The (1994) [Gen. Frank Zane]
82. Black Water (1994)
83. Tom Clancy's 'OP Center' (1995) (TV) [Boroda]
84. In Pursuit of Honor (1995) (TV)
85. Mars Attacks! (1997)
86. Shiloh (1997)
87. Incognito (1997)

Bibliography

Barnouw, Erik. *Tube of Plenty: The Evolution of American Television*, Oxford University Press, New York, 1975

Bergan, Ronald. *Anthony Perkins, A Haunted Life*, Little, Brown and Company, London, 1995

Baker, Carroll. *Baby Doll*, W. H. Allen, London, 1984

Baker, Fred, with Ross Firestone. *Movie People*, Abelard Schuman, London, 1972

Bloom, Claire. *Limelight and After*, Weidenfeld & Nicolson, London, 1982

Bloom, Claire. *Leaving a Doll's House*, Virago, London, 1996

Bordman, Gerald (ed.). *The Oxford Companion to American Theatre*, OUP, Oxford, 1984

Brando, Marlon, with Robert Lindsey. *Songs My Mother Taught Me*, Century, London, 1994

Brewer's Theatre, Cassell, London, 1994

Brown, Les. *Les Brown's Encyclopedia of Television*, 3rd edn, Gale Research, Detroit, 1992

Brownlow, Kevin. *David Lean*, Richard Cohen, London, 1996

Carey, Gary. *Marlon Brando: The Only Contender*, Robson, London, 1985

Chayefsky, Paddy. *Television Plays*, Simon and Schuster, New York, 1955

Clurman, Harold. *The Divine Pastime*, Macmillan, New York, 1974

Coward, Noël. See Payn, Graham and Sheridan Morley

Crist, Judith. *The Private Eye, The Cowboy and the Very Naked Girl*, Paperback Library, New York, 1970

Curtis, Tony, with Barry Paris. *Tony Curtis: The Autobiography*, William Heinemann, London, 1994

Falk, Quentin. *Travels in Greeneland: The Cinema of Graham Greene*, revised edn, Quartet Books, London, 1990

Fay, Stephen. *Power Play: The Life and Times of Peter Hall*, Hodder and Stoughton, London, 1995

Fiore, Carlo. *Bud: The Brando I Knew*, Dell, New York, 1974

Fishgall, Larry. *Burt Lancaster*, Scribners, London, 1995

Henreid, Paul, with Julius Fast. *Ladies' Man*, St Martin's Press, New York, 1984

Hirsch, Foster. *A Method To Their Madness*, W. W. Norton, New York, 1984

Hoskyns, Barney. *Montgomery Clift: Beautiful Loser*, Bloomsbury, London, 1991

Hyams, Joe, with Jay Hyams. *James Dean: Little Boy Lost*, Century, London, 1992

Kazan, Elia. *A Life*, André Deutsch, London, 1988

Levy, Emanuel. *George Cukor, Master of Elegance*, William Morrow, New York, 1994

Manso, Peter. *Brando*, Weidenfeld and Nicolson, London, 1994

Mason, James. *Before I Forget*, Hamish Hamilton, London, 1981

Morley, Sheridan. *James Mason: Odd Man Out*, Weidenfeld & Nicolson, London, 1989

Payn, Graham, and Sheridan Morley (ed.) *The Noël Coward Diaries*, Weidenfeld and Nicolson, London, 1982

Richardson, Tony. *Long Distance Runner*, Faber and Faber, London, 1993

Ross, Lillian and Helen Ross. *The Player: a Profile of an Art*, Simon and Schuster, New York, 1962

Sander, Gordon F. *Serling: the rise and twilight of television's last angry man*, Plume, New York, 1994

Schickel, Richard. *Brando: A Life in Our Times*, Pavilion, London, 1991

Silverman, Stephen M. *David Lean*, André Deutsch, London, 1989

Simon, John. *Private Screenings*, The Macmillan Company, New York, 1967

Spoto, Donald. *Marilyn Monroe*, Chatto & Windus, London, 1993

Stempel, Tom. *Frame Work: A History of Screenwriting in the American Film*, Continuum, New York, 1988

Thomas, Bob. *King Cohn*, Barrie and Rockliff, London, 1967

Walker, John (ed.). *Halliwell's Film Guide* (revised annually), HarperCollins, London, 1994

Walker, John (ed.). *Halliwell's Filmgoer's Companion*, 12th edn., HarperCollins, London, 1997

Winters, Shelley. *Shelley, Also Known As Shirley*, Granada, London, 1981

Winters, Shelley. *The Middle of My Century*, Simon and Schuster, New York, 1989

Zierold, Norman. *The Hollywood Tycoons*, Hamish Hamilton, London, 1969

Zinnemann, Fred. *A Life In The Movies*, Charles Scribner's & Sons, New York, 1992